THE GLOBAL HEART OF DEMOCRACY

SALLY MAHÉ

© 2024 Sally Mahé
All rights reserved
Pointer Oak / Tri S Foundation
First printing. First edition
Edited by Nona Charlston and Michael Ritter
Illustrations by Dan Holmgren and Ben York
Cover and text design by Carl Brune
Printed in the USA
ISBN 979-8-218-50812-8

For people everywhere in the world who are
undertaking unique and courageous responsibility
to fulfill their heart and serve the good of all.

For loving forces, seen and unseen in my life, that
open doors, guide and persistently nudge me to
pursue a deeper understanding of democracy.

For my grandchildren and the next generations of
global citizens — may you use your heart-power to
heal the world with justice, kindness and deep faith.

Foreword

Sally Mahé is a practical visionary whose life demonstrates the principles she espouses. Years ago, she said to me, "Democracy is more than politics," and in this book Sally offers us a clear path to understand and live democracy at many levels, from personal to global to cosmos, as well as from the inside out.

Sally understands, and this book demonstrates, the truth that many find hard to realize; that despite the present destabilizing events in the world that have led to to chaotic conditions, we are living in the midst of a great transition and under the beneficent direction of a deeply spiritual nature that is slowly and surely emerging into outer expression.

She recognizes that we are experiencing a massive shift from a separative reductionist worldview to a unitive interconnected whole system worldview and asks the question, "What would it be like if there really was a cosmic force of love in the universe that holds humanity and guides humanity towards its ultimate fulfillment?"

The fourteen interviews you will experience in *The Global Heart of Democracy* are beautiful and inspiring examples of this regeneration on the planet and the ultimate fulfillment for humanity. They represent the promise of the New Era, the promise of a world that works for everyone and all of life. They demonstrate what policies, programs, education and community decision-making look like done from the perspective of the good of the whole. They offer a glimpse of a Culture of Peace on Earth as we learn to live in right relationship with self, others and all life.

Sally reminds us that we all have a unique contribution to make in this world and that "living on purpose" is at the heart of democracy. In fact, it is at the very heart of life itself, when we offer our best on behalf of the common good. When this becomes a way of life, democracy will naturally be present in politics, education and religion. We will govern and make decisions on behalf of the common good, thereby ensuring that the core needs of all of life are met. Love, Freedom, Beauty and Shared Responsibility reach out and touch our hearts and minds as we read, literally reminding us of our essence, our innate wisdom and the fact of our divine nature. We get a sense of belonging within Life itself as it expresses through myriad forms and in so many ways, all from the one source.

And when Sally says, "How thrilling to speak about democracy as a divine evolutionary process," we want to shout, "yes!" It is about expansion of consciousness. Simply put, democracy means we live through the heart, and in the words of Terry Tempest Williams, "The human heart is the first home of democracy."

We are Cooperators and Co-Creators on this planet and this book sings the song line of our shared destiny, "evolving heart-centered democracy." Enjoy immersing in the hope, the love, the inspiration and the heart-soaring feeling of probability beyond possibility as you embark on this journey with Sally and the fourteen people you will meet from around the world. We are all in this together and joy is a special wisdom.

Thank you, Sally, for sharing your joy, your wisdom, your knowing that democracy is rooted in the human heart, and for naming the freedom we seek to understand and express as the evolutionary impulse carries us forward through these challenging times.

DOROTHY J. MAVER, PHD
June 17, 2024

Dorothy J. Maver is an educator and peacebuilder whose keynote is inspiring cooperation on behalf of the common good. Dot is a co-founder of the Global Silent Minute, the National Peace Academy USA, Global Alliance for Ministries and Infrastructures for Peace, as well as the the Seven Ray Institute.

Dot served as founding executive director of the River Phoenix Center for Peacebuilding (RPCP). She is co-author of the book *Conscious Education: The Bridge to Freedom*.

Sally Mahé

Democracy illuminates a freedom that does not come from the outside but that is rooted in the human heart.

I want people to make democracy their own and meet these times with indomitable spirit and resourcefulness.

Democracy is not only a set of principles enshrined in constitutional systems of government, it is far more than that. It is a universal loving force that opens space for each person to act for the good of all. Democracy illuminates a freedom that does not come from the outside but that is rooted in the human heart.

Terry Tempest Williams wrote, "the human heart is the first home of democracy." As people make consequential choices, moving from fear to love, from acquisition to generosity, from separation to solidarity, from "me" to "we," from hostility to kindness, hearts become full, joy sneaks in, and we understand what being free really means. When we choose to live with that which transcends us, in accord with what gives life, justice and love, the promise of democracy evolves beyond anything it has ever been.

An expanding meaning of the word democracy, loosely translated from the Greek as "people power" (demo/people – kratis/power), is "arising." Bolstered by this awakening love-induced "people power" across the planet, I am passionate to press forward the promise of an evolving heart-centered democracy and keep asking what might be possible for humanity.

I see people all around the world who are truly alive, who are free and living the values that democracy wants for everyone. Usually incognito, without media attention, these people are making courageous decisions to live contrary to the status quo. They are people, not so different than most of us, thoughtful, creative, resourceful, who are moving humanity toward its highest destiny.

As years go by, I've tried to push the words "spiritual democracy" aside, to hide away my inquiries and learning in private journals, but my life events organized around this idea, and this vision of a deeper democracy just kept burning in my heart.

When I was a middle school civics teacher, I saw a unique, divine spark—a genuine gift in each child. I knew then this is what democracy education must elicit! I had to teach the children something more than democratic governing structures and civic responsibility. I saw the children's indomitable spirit, their dreams and possibilities. The promise of democracy provided them with the dignity and the freedom to see themselves at their best and to grow into their life purpose as citizens and contributors to the common good. I was on fire to help these children move toward their potential.

In the early 1990s, a few years after the fall of the Soviet Union, I received a special grant to teach democracy in the new Russia. A Quaker group invited me to speak with elementary school teachers at an alternative school far outside Moscow. The teachers asked me what democracy had to do with personal creativity. They asked, "Can we teach it in kindergarten?" "How does democracy help children value themselves?" I was tingling with excitement! These teachers in a remote area without any direct experience with western democratic government sensed, just like me, that democracy was a force that could elicit the best in the human spirit. Our hearts touched that day. We knew intuitively that democracy had an undiscovered purpose in the world.

A few years later, I became a founding staff member at a global, non-profit organization based in San Francisco, United Religions Initiative (URI). We envisioned that one day URI might become a spiritual cousin of the United Nations, bringing people of the world's diverse religions and spiritual traditions together to work for peace. It was an audacious and seemingly impossible goal in the mid-90s! Early on, I happened to receive a call from Dee Hock, the founder of Visa Card. After leaving Visa, Dee spent several years exploring quantum physics, chaos theory and ancient wisdom. He aimed to regenerate the terms liberty, ethics and civic community in organizations and decided to offer these cutting-edge organizational design ideas to URI.

Dee spoke of creating organizations where people flourished and highest outcomes were realized. He said, "given certain circumstances and the liberty to try, ordinary people will consistently do extraordinary things." Yes! I nearly jumped out of my seat when he told me, "People have the power, they need to see it and to be given the freedom to try!" Again, my heart leapt within me.

After 25 years helping the URI global community develop an organic "bottom-up" way of organizing, my heart is still aflame with the power of people to come together with care and ingenuity to face and solve their problems.

As a nascent global community, we imagined we were giving birth to that which did not yet exist. Ralph Waldo Emerson said, "The power of love, as the basis of a State, has never been tried." Well, this was the time to try to make love and appreciation the basis of a global organization. Maybe it wouldn't happen in our lifetime, but we felt flashes of being what we wanted to become.

In 2003 I was researching ideas that revealed the spiritual qualities of democracy and found the work of Mary Parker Follett, a US thought leader and activist in organizational management theory in the early 20th century. I was overwhelmed by her words:

> There has gradually come into the world a new idea of democracy. If we here tonight pledge ourselves to a new democracy, a new force will be created in the world. For we no longer think of democracy as a form of government. We know now that it is far more than that. It is the substance of our life. It is a flame that burns in the heart of humanity that binds us together and makes us one.

The writings of Mary Parker Follett, Vaclav Havel, Dag Hammarskjold, Jacob Needleman, and other visionary thought leaders presented exciting affirmations of an inner, transcendent meaning of democracy. I decided to learn about a deeper, inner democracy as one would take up a spiritual practice, by reflecting on an inspirational quote each day. I collected 365 quotations, one for each day of the year, and published these in a book, *A Greater Democracy Day by Day*.

Recently, the urge to speak up for this "far out" ideal of democracy has hounded me incessantly. Current threats to democracy in the world are ominous. Today's critical breakdowns also provide opportunities for crucial breakthroughs! The stakes are high. Human beings on planet Earth in the 21st century are facing dark miseries and are worn down by anxieties about what's coming. Will we kill ourselves and most of life on Earth? Will cruel inequality abide? Will we suffer and suffer and suffer? Will we lose our rootedness with our best human qualities—freedom, truth and joy? As we experience the angst of today's world, can we value ourselves enough, band together and accept humanity's divine place in the unfolding story of democracy?

A friend who grew up in the Flint Hills of central Kansas happened to send me a photo of a a heart-shaped stone. There was light sparking from its center. It rested gently in a muddy, gurgling creek. To me, this flint stone was nature's serendipitous gift to this effort. The stone symbolized the global heart of democracy arising from the Earth itself. Out of the muck, out of the rubble, out of the pain, people's life force is awakening. We are learning how to make decisions with our heart, with love.

The rising global heart of democracy is unbounded by nation states and different geographies. What would it be like if there really was a cosmic force of love in the universe that holds humanity and guides humanity towards its ultimate fulfillment?

I reread entries in my journal and felt the awesome tenderness and patience with which my constant queries and doubts were answered by loving guidance from a higher realm of consciousness.

I had intimate conversations with a "voice" I call spiritual democracy. In these journal musings, I personified this spiritual intent of democracy in my imagination and entered a conversation. I wanted to know spiritual democracy intimately. I felt it was yearning to be known and embraced as well. When I shyly asked about its nature, responses came:

I, spiritual democracy, am the process of life embodied by people day by day to make a better world. As people do this, their essential unity — sense of oneness — is awakened.

I am people acting from their truest nature for the benefit of all life.

I am the intrinsic invitation wherein every person is called to fulfill their destiny and act for the common good.

I am, in fact, a divine flow of energy that courses within the soul of every person. As they open to their unique soul intention and act out the unique purpose of their lives, they participate in and create an evolved democratic society.

I am a lively, evolving context that encourages participation, not a noble idea that sits on a pedestal.

How thrilling to speak about democracy as a divine evolutionary process! It is not book-bound or the property of certain people or nations. Mary Parker Follett proclaimed that democracy is so much more than we have understood it to be! Democracy is a loving invitation from divine intelligence to move into a deeper spiritual consciousness, open to the oneness we inhabit with all creation; and it is our invitation to find meaning in our lives as we fulfill our hearts. This new birth of freedom within people's hearts is an "inside job," arrived at through sincere self-learning and in community. It is a revolution in human consciousness.

The Global Heart of Democracy presents interviews with "ordinary" people who are already practicing paths to a deeper democracy. These are people who bring together spiritual commitment with service as local and global citizens. While it is not new that ordinary people, citizens of every country, see a need and selflessly step up to make positive change, it is newsworthy that they are acting with spiritual intent, finding one another and gaining collective momentum. They are deepening their spiritual roots and bravely taking responsibility to create positive change. They are pilgrims finding their way and lighting a path for others. You are invited to discover fourteen individuals whose stories are part of the rising of a counter revolution.

Their stories are rich with examples of a heart-driven democracy and are evidence of the evolving human capacity to contribute to life on Earth. These pilgrims come from many places:

From Audri Scott Williams whose campaign for Congress in Alabama empowered her constituents; Ahmed Shah Karimi transforming his life's calling from Afghanistan to Berlin; Matt Regier, an artist and minister enlivening a small town in Kansas, to three members of the Ariyaratne family cultivating generations of peace and social justice in Sri Lanka.

From James Offuh, a conflict mediator in Cote D-Ivoire; Jon Rasmussen, a trustworthy listener; Biswadeb Chakraborty, a musician peacemaker in West Bengal; Daisy, a thought leader in Vietnam; Audrey Lin, giving away smiles in a service economy; Elisabeth from Austria and Hasan from Syria, a match made in heaven; to Luz, a woman of light, obedient to her ancestors and spirit guides.

Although a miniscule array, like sweet, smiling stars flickering in an immense cosmos of human endeavor, the selections in this book affirm the heroic journey of democracy that is growing in people's hearts. I hope these sparks of light and love inspire you to look around for others who live this way and to look inside and see what is lighting up your own heart.

Create says the sun

I'm sending a river of gold

It is flowing through your heart

Churning the old anew.

The dream is realizing itself upon Earth through you.

Persevere

Victory is near

Perhaps it is here.

—TANYA SABLOCK
Poet, Delhi, India

Audri Scott Williams

The Earth breathes democracy.

We are waking up. What are we waking up to? We are opening up the dream of democracy in new ways. We are waking up both to the governance democracy requires and the participation.

We were sitting in the back parking lot of a forlorn Catholic retreat house in Montgomery, Alabama, the temporary residence and headquarters for our modest campaign team. I had come from California to help my friend Audri in her quest to be elected to the U.S. Congress, representing Alabama's Second District in the Democratic primary election.

Audri, a Native American and African American elder, was a spiritual leader first and a politician second. Her decision to run for office came more from following the guidance of Spirit than political ambition. Rather than strategizing how to win the election, the unspoken questions stirring in us that sultry June evening surfaced: What were we here to learn? What was the deeper journey that brought us together in this moment? Sitting on rickety plastic lawn chairs staring into fading light, Audri calmly said, "The Earth breathes democracy." Her words dropped into my soul. These words were startlingly true.

Audri garnered 40% of the vote and lost the primary in 2018. Years later, Audri reflected on the meaning of her experiences. Audri is one of so many quiet heroes whose life contributes to the evolution of democracy.

S: I want to learn more about how your choice to run for U.S. Congress connects with your understanding of a deeper democracy. What led you into the thicket of politics?

Audri: It began with a friend who asked me, "When are you going to run?" I looked at her like "What?" She said, "You need to run for office." I remember having this sense of, "Well if everybody says 'no.' who's going to run?" If I have an opportunity to run, then I also have the opportunity to shape the conversation. I don't have to do it the way everybody else does it. I could stay true to who I am and breathe that into this particular campaign for Congress.

What was important to me was to define the campaign for myself. I had to look within and ask, "Why am I running? What's important?" And then stay true to those answers and not be pulled into parroting a prescribed party slate to win.

I wanted to come from the concerns of the people. My goal was to find out the issues that were important to people in my district and ask myself, "How can I lend voice to those concerns?" We're talking about concerns from what is known in Alabama as the Black Belt, which was once a major area of slavery here—growing cotton and peanuts and so forth. Today one of the major concerns is that there is not enough industry here to support people's livelihoods. Industries that used to be here moved out because of redistricting. There is raw sewage on the ground. Children are playing in it like it's a little pond. There is low opportunity for folks to have a job that sustains them.

If we're going to have a democracy, we've got to make sure that people have basic opportunities to live a quality life and are free to make choices that lead to that. For me, it wasn't as critical to win as it was to be a voice that represented the needs of the people. This was how I could extend my spiritual practice of peace and justice.

S: As I handed out "vote for Audri flyers" at shopping centers, I witnessed people waking up to something they never thought possible. African American women beamed. When they met you, a kind of democracy that included them lit them up. During the campaign, did you experience breakthrough moments that went beyond the goal of winning?

Audri: I had that experience so much! I remember when we went to the voting polls, people would just reach out and grab me. I don't think it had anything to do with me, the person that I am. It was the acknowledgment that there had not been a person of color running for office from that district since the 1800s during Reconstruction. John Rapier was his name. He ran for Congress and won.

People were energized by a woman of color on the ticket. That was very inspiring. Our little campaign team took a while to get the engine going, but by the time we got to election time we had a lot of momentum; recognition was growing.

S: **You told me how important it is to bring in the voices of the ancestors to help us go beyond where we think we can go. Please say more about that.**

Audri: As a child I was taught always to honor the ancestors. There is an energy, a dynamic force that is accessible to all of us if we open ourselves. The ancestors are waiting to be called in—in support of what we are doing; to join us in our obstacles and in our victories.

I happened to grow up with some very awesome elders. My mentor was Amelia Boynton Robinson. She was beaten down in 1965 in that first attempt to cross the Selma Bridge for voting rights on the march to Montgomery. It was her picture in the paper that ignited people and sustained the walk. She continued to walk until they made it across that bridge.

To me, ancestral energy is palpable. I've always been taught that the ancestors are just waiting for us to reach out. They want to hold us in that sacred way which is beyond the conversations we have about race, or what's good—what's bad. It's pure energy.

In fact, I feel this ancestral energy right now. I'm working on a project called Redemption Voyage. We are taking 18 people, ages 18 to 28—nine men, nine women. They are going to sail from Charleston, South Carolina to Senegal; then come down what's called the Slave Coast from Senegal to Benin, and then cross the ocean from Benin back to the Bay of Mobile where we're going to end the journey. It's a six-month commitment. One of the elders asked me, "Maybe it's too dangerous for them to be on a ship. Why don't you fly them over?"

Well, the vision I had was of these young people on a ship. So, I prayed. I called on my ancestors. "This is a big undertaking, and I don't want to get in the way of the best decision." I just asked them, "Will they be safe?" I was in that meditative state. Then I saw it! The vision! Every time I think of it—"Wooo! I saw these brown hands, from the bottom of the ocean, reaching up—because, you know, millions died on the journey over. I saw these hands holding the hull of the boat, just passing it over the water, hand to hand, from east to west, the whole way." I said, "Fine—this is the call." With the campaign, I saw the possibility of winning, but by listening to the ancestors I was guided to see that what was more important were the conversations.

S: **What do you want to achieve with your new project, Redemption Voyage? How do you see it contributing to a deeper democracy?**

Audri: In America we struggle with racism, particularly here in the South. It's always a loaded conversation. There's anger, frustration and fear on one side. Guilt, shame and blame on the other. How do we get beyond shame and blame? How do we get beyond who's guilty, who's not guilty?
We can come from a sacred space and say, "It's time for change." Instead of doing things that don't make a difference, how can we enter into sacred space and listen? How can we bring ourselves into a place of true democracy which includes listening to the voices of the people, the voices of the Earth, and the voices of the cosmos?

The Redemption Voyage is about that kind of change. It is having our young people go back as a symbolic return and to be welcomed home to Africa. The deeper healing and prayer is for the return of the ancestors. It is an expression of freedom and a symbolic return to Africa. It is a fulfillment of the prophecy of many of the African villages that one day their descendants would return. Once you have that sort of acknowledgment— the healing of that ship coming back in freedom represents the new journey. That's the true freedom!

There are so many things that influence a decision that you don't recognize in the moment. You don't realize that these experiences are setting you up for something important. You don't really realize it until suddenly you have an ahah! moment.

I was in Benin on Whydah Beach, which was where the slave ship, the Clotilda, departed to go to Mobile Harbor. In 1865, slavery was illegal in the U.S., but an Alabama boat builder made a bet that he could smuggle in more Africans even though it was illegal.

I had a very profound experience on Whydah Beach. That night I was just pushed to go out and sleep on the beach. What happened is that I heard drums around 2–3 o'clock in the morning and I heard people praying. When I looked around, I didn't see anybody. The next day, I was telling our guide what happened, and he said that there is a house not far from that beach where people have been praying an unbroken prayer ever since the first Africans were taken as slaves from Benin.

This Redemption Journey is bringing back freedom. What are we bringing back? We are bringing back freedom! We are releasing the heavy history … it's like another end of slavery. We are releasing "enslavement" for all people. We are redeeming this whole process so we can go forward.

You asked me what I wanted this journey to achieve. What I want is to be welcomed back to Africa … then sent back to America in the glory of freedom!

The calling we face is to heal more deeply than we have before. I look at where the political system is right now, and it's sick. To me, it mirrors the challenges facing the Earth herself.

The Redemption Journey is one way we are recovering, celebrating and giving honor to our sacred truths, the truths of who we are. It's critical to see how we can transcend where we are and do better.

The voice of the "beloved community" needs to be heard. The "beloved community," like spiritual democracy, speaks to the collective good we can bring to each other and to the Earth. I think that, ultimately, this is what we are here to learn—as long as it takes. I don't think human beings can get off the hook by becoming extinct. I believe this is humanity's work, and until we get it, we're going to keep having an opportunity to revisit what this means. The Earth is speaking loud and clear now. My prayer is that we wake up enough to hear her, so she doesn't have to make it any clearer.

S: **You have said that the beloved community calls forth the latent spiritual capacity in people to embrace interrelatedness and live for the benefit of one another. Where are the guides, the teachers to help this happen?**

Audri: I've been envisioning an aspen forest and the amazing work of mycelia. The Earth mirrors us and we mirror the Earth. I've been observing and meditating on the connective tissues in all dimensions and how powerfully sustaining these fibers are at every level.

S: **A mycelia network in a forest is such a good example! It's the epitome of sacred democracy: the connection of "as above, so below" or "as within, so without"—we are all a part of this connective tissue.**

Audri: Maybe our separation is just an illusion. Maybe who we think we are is an illusion that interferes with the truth of who we really are: a part of this system that is our sacred Earth that includes us. We're a part of the whole rather than these separate pieces. We come together in this synergistic energy, and we find that we are one with it all.

S: That's a powerful awakening.

Audri: It's the matrix. We can define it as the ancestors, or as the angels, or in any of those ways. I like to think that we are each sacred and can use our sacred wisdom in any way we choose. We have forgotten who we are.

I think humanity's journey is probably evolving exactly the way it should and it's inevitable. I think whether we are billions of people on the planet, or whether we end up being a few million people on the planet, this is humanity's ultimate journey.

The Earth is righting herself. In that righting the consciousness we hold has to be affected as well. Whether we are aware of it or not, is not as important as the fact that we are beginning to think differently. We are beginning to ask different questions. We are reshaping the dialogue, even to the point of looking at who we are and continuing to ask that question.

Our human voices will begin to harmonize with the voice of the Earth and the cosmos. It will be one voice, not necessarily one word, but a voice. It will be a harmony. We are going through a harmonizing period.

Maybe it's going to be a musical journey—who knows what it might be? As the Earth is breathing, we are breathing with it. We are allowing ourselves to be a part of that spiritual exchange that comes from the people speaking words of truth. Maybe that is how we will begin to get the message more and more.

S: Thank you for your wisdom, Audri. I agree that an emerging sacred democracy is bound up with human beings learning to live as a "beloved community." As long as it takes and with whatever calamities that befall the human race along the way, people, all of us together, are destined to take this journey. As people of Earth, our responsibility is to live in harmony with Earth and make decisions that build confidence and support one another's fullest potential. Simply and mysteriously, the Earth breathes a vibration that invites humanity to do its part.

About Audri

Audri recently served as the Spiritual Director of the Spiritual Enrichment Center in Dothan, Alabama, an open and diverse community that encourages new ways for people to know, feel and express their true nature and to honor the oneness with all life.

I first met Audri as she was completing the Trail of Dreams World Peace Walk with a small group of peace pilgrims who she described as people who never thought they would come together but undertook this global walk for peace because they knew they could make a difference.

In her book, *Awakening the Heart of the Beloved Community*, Audri supports her vision of an evolving beloved community that includes all life and that is needed for a sustainable future. Audri is guided by a mystical lineage of indigenous grandmothers and ancestors who are close at hand to guide humanity and show what is possible.

A memory about Audri that sticks with me is during her campaign for U.S. Congress, just before election day, when Audri decided to leave Montgomery and take her campaign team to cross the Edmund Pettus Bridge in Selma, Alabama. Rather than spending the last crucial day pamphletting key neighborhoods in Montgomery, she chose to honor Amelia Boynton Robinson and all the civil rights marchers who set out across that bridge on what history recounts as Bloody Sunday. By listening to her heart- voice, Audri was guided by a deeper wisdom. A global heart that lives within us and reaches to the transcendent is awakening across the planet. Audri remains loyal to its promise.

We need ancestors. We need people to lift our gaze and show us what is possible. This [uplift] helps unleash global innovation on many fronts. The experience in 1965 crossing the Selma Bridge was an event that was a collective piercing of the veil . . . something that we could do as people of color. Amelia Boynton Robinson said that what gave her and the other marchers courage was that we knew we had already won. We had to be strong enough to carry it out.

AIR FORCE VETERAN
AUDRI SCOTT WILLIAMS
WE ARE THE CHANGE!
VOTE JUNE 5
Adams graduates law school

Ahmad Shah Karimi

When we feel ourselves a part of something bigger,
we find belongingness.

I know that each of us, from every part of the world, has something of value to bring to other cultures. We can see ourselves bigger than the society or the local identity that we are born into.

In August 2021, as the Taliban swept into power in Afghanistan, Ahmad and his staff feared for their lives if they stayed. Miraculously, they were guided to safe passage through Kabul, to a specific gate at the airport and onto a plane just hours before bombs blasted that same airport gate. Making the heart-wrenching decision to leave family and the land he cherished, Ahmad and 11 staff from the organization he started, Afghanistan Youth Empowerment and Peacebuilding Organization (AYEPO) became refugees in Berlin.

A few years before, just after Ahmad had launched AYEPO, he shared with me how his mother instilled a commitment to hard work and bringing benefit to others. He said, "Through her love and belief in me I believed in myself and wanted to make my mom feel good. Her presence and wisdom taught me to have confidence in what women can do, which carried over to AYEPO's commitment to women's empowerment."

Ahmad inspires people to make critical choices about their identity. "I know that each of us, from every part of the world, has something of value to bring to other cultures. We can see ourselves bigger than the society or the local identity that we are born into. Becoming an agent of peace starts on the inside of us with a sense of having a bigger identity. When people see that they are not limited to one place or one culture, they find a bigger identity and the world gets closer. When we feel ourselves a part of something bigger, we find belongingness. This helps us do the good we want to do."

No one I know is experiencing loss and soul-shaking more than Ahmad. His way of being human, especially in tough times, is a light for the world that will never be hidden.

S: It is wonderful to be with you, Ahmad. I want this exploration to bring attention to people who are living true to their purpose.

Let's begin with a question about the organization you founded. Before the Taliban takeover in 2021, AYEPO gathered hundreds of young adults to experience peace leadership education. In those first years, what achievements stick with you?

Ahmad: Thank you so much for including me in this conversation. As you talk with wonderful individuals along this journey toward a deeper democracy, wisdom, good inspirations and experiences will emerge. Regarding AYEPO, there are many memories.

The moment I started, it was a winter day, snowy. I wondered if participants would show up because the snow was deep. Just a few showed up, but it was enough to get started. I was excited with the prospects. I regarded this first day not as one session only but a beginning that had the potential to go very far. Later, it did, along with challenges and everything. There were challenges on a personal level, particularly for me because I had the privilege of spearheading the organization.

In the course of our journey, there were so many activities. Sometimes, they were designed to delve into specific topics to reach intended outcomes; but, especially at the beginning, we were just trying things out to see what we could do.

At first, we did not have intentions to have specific results-oriented programs. We just wanted to bring people together and give them a shared space where they could learn about each other, talk together and share stories.

Through that process we also offered skills that would help them see practical application in their school studies and in their lives. That was at the beginning.

Later, the organization grew and expanded. I thought, "Yeah! Hey! We need to think beyond our own community and reach out to young people across the country." I knew that a lot of responsibility would come with that, which indeed it did.

To answer your question about achievements, sometimes I find it hard to call what we did "achievements"… because it is something you do and then there is something else to do. It is a continuous journey. It's not like you look towards a mountain and just aim to reach it. It's not like that. When you reach one mountain, you see that there is a mountain behind that mountain, and there are more and more mountains. Sometimes you see they are low and sometimes they are high. In the process of climbing these mountains, it is wonderful. You inhale it, you cherish it, celebrate it and then you let it go because you see there is another mountain that is farther away. You realize you are going to keep going to reach there.

S: **I love that analogy of the mountains beyond the mountain. Can you tell us about an experience of this?**

Ahmad: In the beginning I shared the vision with a number of people, but I was the only one organizing everything. Other people came along later. Bringing a group of people together at the beginning was a first milestone. Getting a legal license to get the organization started was pretty easy. To keep it going is something difficult.

Leading an organization run by volunteers brings challenges because some people may not be a perfect match. Besides, you cannot force people to work because they are not paid employees. One must ignite a passion in them for the work and what they can accomplish when they join forces.

I wanted to create something that would bring all the people together. I'm surprised looking back, how I was able to bring people with different interests and abilities together. Everyone wanted to contribute something. Of course, there were moments when we had challenges. We had arguments. Some people came and some people left, but it was still wonderful. So many young people came together so they could be part of this and feel this passion and this excitement. That is one thing.

Another thing that I feel about the organization is that there was a sense of bonding, of friendship, a sense of purpose that was present among the team. This feeling went beyond us as team members and affected the participants. The participants could see us, feel our genuine friendship and we could see this feeling growing among them as well. At the beginning, we were doing small things but there was a lot of excitement. Everyone wanted to take part, either as a participant, a volunteer, or as a team member. Just wanting to be part of it all was the energy present there.

There is one program I vividly remember. We had a three-day program for high school students. On the first day, we had training in communication, listening, problem solving and drawing. On the third day, the participants had to go and try to transfer their new skills to a group of orphans located in a suburb of Kabul. When we entered the orphanage, I could feel everyone's anxiety and nervousness. We divided the participants into groups so that each group would do something with the kids. In a little while, the sense of anxiety gave way to laughter and smiles. Each group was busy: dancing, playing guitar, writing, drumming. There was so much going on. The orphans were happily clutching the hands of our team members and participants. There was a positive, whole flow of energy there.

It occurred to me that maybe this was one of the better days that the orphans ever had. They felt so special, so cared for and loved that day. Maybe they didn't have a father or a mother or any family member, but in that moment, it seemed that all of their tensions and worries drifted away, and they were wholly present. It is natural for children to live in the moment, but things can happen that cause tension and push them away from being present.

Each of us created everything. Our team brought that kind of energy and ambience to the participants and then they took it forward with the orphans. We all were immersed into the whole experience — forgetting personalities and problems. It was something like that. Everyone was overjoyed, shouting, playing and clapping. It was wonderful!! The children shared poems, stories, outpourings of emotions and tears. The orphans had tapped into something personal; some fought to hold their feelings back and some couldn't. Some let go of things that they had been holding. It was an unforgettable day!

S: Those children will keep that experience very much as a part of who they are forever. You were the director, but you valued teamwork and developed team spirit to move AYEPO's work forward. How did the AYEPO team work together?

Ahmad: At the beginning I shared the vision and asked them, "do you want to be part of this or not?" Voluntary work was something that felt exciting even though in Afghanistan it was a bit foreign. Even so, everyone was excited to do something and to be part of it.

I asked them: how are we going to do this? Each idea was listened to, each person felt acknowledged. Each person brought something to the table. Young women said how much they were moved to see how each person was valued, and each voice mattered.

We were able to do these things in this way because each person brought something. One had the energy, one had the idea, one had the creativity. We saw that each one of us was able to do something. I would see who was good at what and assign them the tasks. They were given the freedom to create in their own ways.

Mostly, I cherish what I did in the organization. I made sure that each person was validated. They could go and do something that gave them personal satisfaction. Then, as a team, we felt that increased sense of purpose, and as an organization we could feel that. We would give participants space to find what they are good at and then they would go do it. That is something.

S: Yes, it is something! You speak of the fact that if you want to teach skills and help people see their unique value, it's important that each person becomes involved in their own transformation. Is there more you want to say about those days with AYEPO in Afghanistan?

Ahmad: Those were wonderful days. Challenges and surprises happened all along the way, and we received the support we needed. In the beginning we didn't have funding and we just started with the idea that I had a job and that somehow, I could support the organization through that.

Then we designed a project, and we received some money and we just said, "ok guys, let's go and do our idea"… and we just went ahead and did it. We just kept going and it showed us how we could carry out activities and how far we could go. It was beautiful, the changes that we could see happening. The Peace Camp that we did in June 2021 a few months before the collapse was such a transformation. We brought young people from across the country together. So many stories of change and transformation came from that experience!

There was one guy who was very introverted and did not engage in conversation. But at the end of the camp, he had a smile on his face. He had changed. Like him there were individuals who spoke about the shifts they had experienced. One said that elders in his community had negative perceptions about people from other ethnic groups. During Camp, he acknowledged that what he had been told about other ethnic groups was not right. He said meeting young people from other groups was a testimony to the fact that when spaces are created where people are allowed to simply engage in conversation, not to be told how to think, change happens. One conversation would lead to another and to another. They would come to see that even with their differences, they are one. That kind of attitude change was experienced to a great extent.

It was a very exciting program. We were expecting that the participants would go on to do similar things within their own communities. But that dream was cut short. That's the way I would say it for lack of a better description.

S: The story about the man who shifted his view reminds me of a quote you gave me once. I have used your quote to help people understand the significance of expanding one's identity. You said, "When people see that they are not limited to one place or one culture, they find a bigger identity and the world gets closer. When we feel ourselves a part of something bigger, we find belongingness. This helps us do the good we want to do."

I think this is key to reversing cycles of hate and violence. Please tell me more about how you came to realize that this statement is true for people.

Ahmad: On a trip to an Indian ashram, I saw people from different corners of the world. The meditations and the services there created a whole ambience and energy for bringing diverse peoples together. People were coming together and celebrating something that transcends the individual's identity, the notion of self that we usually hold onto.

I felt this idea started there. I had the sense of connecting, not only with other people but also to the world around us, to all of life. One life form is no different than another. We might not see ourselves as similar beings, but that sense of connection is there.

Everywhere you go, in Afghanistan or other countries, you see people no matter what background they come from, or what name they give to God, no matter what they practice or what they don't practice, you recognize that there is something there that people share in common.

The nature of the problems might be different but the sorrow or fear or worry that is felt is the same. In Afghanistan, for example, it might be the lack of peace, lack of security, the presence of poverty. In other places, people might struggle with other issues. One sees how much connects us and that should help bring us together.

It is like a tree that is rooted into the earth. We are part of each other and part of the earth.

I feel there might come a day when people will forget about the local identities that separate us. Individuals may take pride in who they are and, at the same time, feel truly connected with people who don't share their language, culture, nationality and so on.

S: I believe that expanding one's identity is key to the evolution of humanity. Do you think it's possible for people to hold both of these ways of thinking: to say, "I'm proud of my culture and my country—and—I identify with people in other cultures?"

Ahmad: I think it's a possibility. Whether it will happen or not, or when it happens is uncertain. It is wonderful to hope for and dream for this. What one envisions may not come into reality in one's lifetime. It may take generations for it to happen. But you can see that it is happening here and there, and that people are transitioning from a smaller identity to this kind of broader identity, to something beyond.

I see that our connection with Mother Earth can bring about a realization that we are all related. We might consider that this is "just nature," or, it's "just animals and trees." We might continue to see that everything is built for our benefit and destroy it all. But we need to realize that all these things live not for our benefit, that they have their own lives.

I think it might be possible for people to change, but it feels like this kind of change needs to happen on an individual level. It may be that people will eventually realize that the only way to fight the issues of security, climate and other things is to come together. Looking at the state of the world now, it is difficult to say what is possible. Every day there are more signs and more ways that people try to hurt each other and to destroy everything. It begins on an individual level. Someone standing up for a cause and along the way others join and slowly it becomes a giant movement of change.That is how it starts. I say that from experience.

S: With AYEPO, you created situations where the young people began to extend their identity beyond their perspective of coming from this tribe or this set of values. What did you do to get that to happen?

Ahmad: It is easy and difficult at the same time. Sometimes we can create a space, but some conversation may go poorly, or conversations might result in something we couldn't predict.

Some of the programs had a set of questions that asked participants to say their name, where they come from and then list the challenges in their community. Many had similar problems and needs. One would say, "we want peace, we want education." These kinds of responses would create a sense of common need.

They might share a story about something that moved them—about their life, their parents, their first day of school. That act of sharing is what moved and created a bond between them. Sometimes they were surprised when they said something that they would share only with a best friend, but now they were sharing that with a stranger. Just creating a place for people to share is one thing.

Some may believe that there is diversity in universities. But everyone still has their own lives there. They carry prejudices about other people, and they don't really listen to others in those places. They still see the other person based on their own image. There are not too many opportunities for them to sit and really delve into difficult topics—about the past, the conflicts and how to heal. They would have already drawn their conclusion: this person is different or that person is not good. When people really come together and talk, that old image fades away and a new image can replace it.

S: That sounds kind of easy as you explain it but it's really a radical education to bring people together with this intent.

Ahmad: Before AYEPO, I had not formally studied much about peace. We were offering these experiences just operating from a good intention, a good heart. We were just coming from a feeling inside of ourselves and creating that space for others. It was wonderful to see the friendships that were created and how people went on to do their own things, going off on their own and taking up challenges like cleaning up their city or other initiatives.

S: Sadly, since 2021 Afghanistan is under such repression and economic hardship. Is there a way for you and your team in Germany to continue the work?

Ahmad: When I landed in Berlin some colleagues in Kabul continued to do activities for the girls there. We started these activities in October 2021. We continued to organize leadership training, psycho-social support and other capacity building training. We never stopped.

But lately, we had to stop because new restrictions are preventing women from going to school or university. We are brainstorming ideas about how to move on, about how to continue our programs.

For boys, we are able to continue programs, but we are thinking about how to do this for girls and women. We are running activities with support from one of my friends in Kabul. I am supporting him and his team with efforts like providing funds and introducing them to trainers to help them do their work. There is an amazing peacebuilder in Australia who supports our peace efforts along with his friends.

This is not something big, it is more like a few drops in the ocean. One of our intentions was just to create a shared space. This is especially important because so many of these young girls and women are feeling lonely and isolated.

We created an opportunity where people come and share and so many stories have emerged. Some say, "Oh, I was at home, and I felt it was just me going through these feelings, now I know that others are like me. Now I don't feel lonely." The young women became united around a collective pain and a collective vision for a better future.

There is a collective pain that they are going through but there is a collective vision: for education, for freedom, for democracy and for the values they had been acquainted with during the last 20 years. AYEPO has not stopped.

S: **It sounds like no matter how dangerous the repression, the determination in the young women is strong. Are there indicators that they will succeed in determining their lives?**

Ahmad: It's crucial to acknowledge the current situation of women in Afghanistan while considering ways to support them. Despite facing bleak circumstances and being marginalized in society, women remain resilient and hopeful about the future. There's a palpable sense of determination within them, manifesting in their dreams of a future filled with freedom and opportunities for education, work and the kind of life they desire.

I believe that change is possible in Afghanistan, though it may take time. I think it is also up to the men in the country to stand alongside women and fight for that change. And generally, all people need to put their differences aside, mobilize forces and carve out a shared future—one synonymous with equality, rather than one in which one group or ethnicity holds power while the rest are sidelined. It should be a future where all members of society—women, youth and ethnic or religious minorities— have a part in shaping it.

After the Taliban takeover, women of Afghanistan courageously took to the streets, fearlessly demonstrating their demands. Their voices resounded with clarity and strength, echoing a unified message: bread, work, freedom. They demonstrated in the face of brutal reprisals from the Taliban—ranging from beatings to arrests, torture and even death. I believe that speaks volumes about their courage and determination. While their basic rights are currently stripped away, it's important to recognize that regimes are transient. An oppressive regime like the Taliban may attempt to silence them, but it cannot extinguish their spirit or their hopes for a better life.

The women will keep going and fighting for their rights in the face of challenges until a new and hopefully brighter era dawns. When it does, women and girls should be an integral part of it, because they started the movement and protested for their rights. We cannot simply expect the politicians and the leaders who fled to come back and rule the country again. They failed us. They betrayed us. They put their own interests before the people they claimed they serve.

Women should spearhead the government or whatever structure emerges when democracy resurfaces in Afghanistan. Given the fact that it is a patriarchal society, it is hard to see that this would happen, at least anytime soon. My hope and wish are that eventually someday there will be an era like this – one in which women have a meaningful role in the government. Because no team can win when half of its members are on the bench.

S: I pray that the indomitable human spirit will eventually gain collective force and a new era will emerge. I trust that this new era will come because the seeds are planted in human beings to live into those values.

Ahmad, you are a person who lives with pain in terms of the change that has come into your life. If you feel comfortable sharing, how do you tap into the strength needed to keep going?

Ahmad: To be honest, sometimes it is very difficult. I find it hard to describe and realize. Life is a journey, and it goes on. Problems are part of it. Sometimes, one would find it easy to move on in the aftermath of something that has had the potential to change everything.

Perhaps one could get so used to a certain place, a certain culture that it would be difficult to move on from there. I make a conscious effort to keep what needs to be kept and let go of other things. Though home is a physical place, it can also be a feeling one would carry with oneself wherever one goes.

At times, when I look back at home, away from family and the community and witnessing so much suffering there, it breaks my heart. Although I try to help in whatever way I can, I also accept the fact that I am far from home now, and I need to move forward. I believe I am heading in that direction. Establishing oneself in a new environment and culture, and discovering new dreams and aspirations, takes time.

In terms of strength, to tell the truth I don't know what gives me strength other than there is this life. It flows, and you've got to flow with it. I might say to myself that my family's situation will change for the better. It may change. It may not. So, I don't hold onto that.

Sometimes I cry, sometimes I laugh, sometimes I dance. Sometimes I am not able to sleep and sometimes I fall asleep in a matter of minutes. Life just keeps on going. No one knows when one's brief role play will end.

S: **Thank you for speaking from your heart. What you are saying is wise: trust life to flow. We don't create the flow; we flow with it. When suffering is with us, don't push it away. Allow it. We can learn to be with pain and feel compassion with people all over the world.**

Thank you for living each day in the flow you find yourself in. You have my love and deep respect.

Ahmad: Yes. Thanks so much.

S: **One last note, can you share any "green shoots," any sparks of possibility rising—good things breaking through in the midst of suffering?**

Ahmad: Especially with the situation in Afghanistan, there are many people, young people especially, I am thinking about women and girls. People are stepping up and organizing mentorship programs and other activities and ways to support families.

People are waking up and doing a lot of things to connect with others and doing things for others. Even if they don't feel the pain themselves, they can imagine it and that should inspire them to act, in whatever capacity they can from wherever they are in the world. That is something to behold.

Acknowledging the situation of people in Afghanistan, or anywhere in the world, is important. Equally important is to do something about it. Because there is no other way.

S: What if the evolution of this deeper democracy comes through the broken heart, the wounded heart? Will it be suffering that moves humanity to a better place?

Ahmad: Yes, that's true. Listening to that heart, connecting with others, creating spaces and opportunities where people share and spend time together is such a good way.

In a world where there is technology and innovation there is so much that fills our lives. Sometimes it is hard to find the time to spend a moment with oneself. That is a challenge. If people would reach out and connect with each other and slowly, slowly that would create a different era, a different future. It may not happen soon, but these small things can make a big difference.

S: I see people speaking from a heart-centered place—sharing from their deepest pain and sharing joys, the glory of a bird singing in the morning.

Thank you, Ahmad. It has been a blessing to be with you in this conversation.

Ahmad: Thank you for the opportunity. I went into this conversation without any preparation. I do that often. Sometimes it goes well and sometimes not. I just go with what emerges spontaneously in the moment and trust that. Sometimes it just flows, and sometimes it doesn't. I hope that this conversation fell close to answering the questions.

S: Your responses were excellent. We are connected in a process of discovery, and I trust that what emerges will contribute to the journey.

About Ahmad

Before launching AYEPO, Ahmad was involved in organizations working on human rights, democratic values, Afghan art and culture and healing the environment. He realized that youth were a valuable untapped resource but because of decades of war in Afghanistan the youth had lived lives shaped by violence and conflict. He decided to find ways for youth to see themselves as peace ambassadors who could heal communities in practical ways and get healed themselves.

AYEPO created places where young people from different tribal groups learned how to work together, mobilize around ideas for positive changes in their own communities, and where they could create a larger vision for Afghanistan. Youth received peace education, leadership and skills in learning from one another.

In Berlin, Ahmad keeps the vision of what's possible burning in his heart for himself and others. He yearns for people around the world who care about basic freedoms and economic wellbeing for the people in Afghanistan to take action. Shared heartbreak can mobilize solidarity. He is completing a memior to share his personal story; to keep open the paths for what's possible; and to uplift the generosity in the hearts of Afghan people and the beauty of their culture.

People are waking up and doing a lot of things to connect with others and do things for others. Even if they are not able to feel the pain themselves, they can imagine it and step up and do things. Maybe that is the start of a good thing. Wherever they are in the world they start doing things for others.

Matt Regier

Matt, Tia, Eliot and Lyda arrived in town
as if by divine appointment.

Basically, [culture] means the nurturing of natural growth. You can see this if you look at yogurt or cheese. You look at "cultures;" the idea is that you are taking something in nature and nurturing it, you are directing its growth in some way, to serve a human purpose.

Matfield Green, a tiny town of 50 inhabitants, lies in the heart of Chase County, Kansas, in the midst of the tallgrass prairie. If you fold a map of the lower 48 states in quadrants, Chase County is at heart-center of the U.S. Matt, his wife Tia and their two young children, Eliot and Lyda, arrived in town as if by divine appointment. The town is turning around—their affection is making a difference.

The community church was being fought over. Some townsfolk wanted to transform it into a venue for concerts and lectures. People argued about its future. Although Matt and Tia were planning to manage an art gallery nearby, they instead chose to serve the church with Matt as minister and Tia as music director of the flailing Matfield Green Community Church and to adopt a dilapidated school.

I met Matt and Tia for the first time at a Sunday Service. With a diverse handful of local folks that morning, I felt at home, respected and inspired. I felt that the same mystery that pulled me to the tallgrass prairie some years earlier was flowing with humble grace here in this small-town community. An artist, minister and community leader, Matt's religious foundation, gentle wisdom and conviction to enrich rural culture at the heart of America lit up my soul.

S: Thank you, Matt, for joining me on this quest for a deeper democracy. I want to lift up the stories of people around the world who embody core spiritual values and committed civic engagement. I'm grateful to be speaking with you today.

I would like to begin with your story. Were there experiences in your upbringing that helped you take the path that you are on and that brought you to where you are today?

Matt: It's tricky in a way. I struggled through some of my later childhood or adolescence. I didn't do particularly well in school. I had poor attention span and focus, and I often lost interest in what we were doing. I struggled to find friends for a while.

It was toward the end of high school and going to college where I started to have a sense that I was connecting with some latent desires and visions that I didn't quite have language and experience for.

I didn't grow up in a household with things like art or literature, or a lot of book reading. I grew up on a corn farm. Education was important but not necessarily to discover thought or artistic creation.

It was a pragmatic, rural culture. It was a small Mennonite community in Nebraska; a rich community. And, like others it was fairly insular and occasionally rigid, I guess.

I had friends who read more than I did. I remember encountering books, large libraries, bookstores and coffee shops,that opened up my world. I began to explore deeper intellectual questions and creative endeavors. In small, farming towns that is usually the moment when you leave your agricultural background, move to the city and don't look back.

Eventually, after further study and especially through encountering writers like Wendell Berry, I began to rethink what a return to the land and to a rural community would be like.

It was a kind of awakening. It made me want to broaden my experience and perspective but also to ask what I could offer in return. I think it was Wendell Berry who asked, "what does it look like to bring something back in return?" It was not actually a return to the community of my birth. I didn't do that, but Tia and I did return to a rural community.

S: What drew you back? What did Wendell Berry inspire that made you want to live in rural America?

Matt: Partly, it was recognizing the need, the sense of lack. The path that I was on after college and then after seminary, headed me towards academia and teaching. That kind of career, although good and understandable, tends towards being mobile, moving to the next position and is not necessarily suited to putting down roots. You have to go where the jobs are, if there are jobs. It does not necessarily connect to where the need is. Most of the jobs were in places that were more intellectually, culturally and economically developed.

The need is in places where economies are struggling, where the cultural resources have been depleted and where creative resources have also been depleted. In my case, I'm talking about rural communities. But it could be other places too, maybe inner-city areas or smaller metropolitan areas or whatever.

It was that motivation as well as acknowledging my emotional, spiritual feelings and the connection with the land that I formed as a child … the sense of the open space around me. I grew up surrounded by corn fields. There was very little wilderness or wild places to speak of but there was a deep sense of being under a massive sky. Just the sense of orienting myself in a very large open space got into my spiritual consciousness. I wanted to reconnect with these aesthetic and spiritual experiences.

S: I'm touched when you say, where the need is the greatest is where life can be so meaningful. We're not taught that it is out of the way places where exciting and creative things happen. How did your artwork emerge in these circumstances? How does your spiritual connection to the land express itself?

Matt: I didn't have any sense of the heritage of art. I hadn't visited a gallery or an art museum until, I'm not sure when, but closer to when I was going to college. But my elder brother was really good at drawing; he had an ability and passion for drawing and I think he passed that down to me. He started drawing and I started drawing. Drawing became an important part of my childhood and something that I could do when I was failing to pay attention in class. It had therapeutic value to me that way. I started to leave it behind later in high school. In college I took a few classes in art history, but that still didn't make it a part of my vocation.

It was later when I was in seminary that I started developing a great appreciation for wood cuts and block prints. I found books of different kinds of art, literature, poetry, essays. I would see these plain black and white woodcuts and engravings, and I just started to wonder how these are made. Essentially, I tried to teach myself how to make block prints, woodcuts, or linocuts. Through a series of trial and error I developed a degree of proficiency in making linocuts, which is like a wood cut but made with what is called "artist linoleum" (a block of saw dust made with linseed oil that is used like a block of wood). You carve into this block, then you ink up its surface, creating something like a stamp that you use to print an image. Various levels of complexity can be built up from there.

I got into printmaking mainly on my own and have since connected with other printmakers. Especially when we moved back to Kansas, it became a way for me to explore, observe and translate the surface of the ground, the visual surface of the prairie as I saw it.

It's interesting that looking out on the prairie to an untrained eye, there's grass. Depending on the time of the year, people wouldn't know the difference between a prairie and a wheat field. But the difference is vast and complex. The prairie itself is only 60–80% grass and there might be more than a dozen kinds of grasses and more than hundreds of different kinds of plants. Even beyond that complexity on the surface, there is the deeper complexity of the roots underneath which are the real core of the prairie. The roots are preserved through the seasons when the surface dies off.

The closer you observe, the longer you train yourself to look carefully at the prairie you can see, even at a distance; what kinds of plants are growing? What is the balance? Why is it taller over here? Why is it shaggier? Why is it this color? What do the plants look like in this color or from this distance?

Initially what looks like such a simple, minimalist landscape, a hillside, a more or less flat expanse, holds all kinds of treasures and complexities the further and deeper you look into it.

Through my printmaking and through the density of mark making and through subtle variations in the lines that are created through the cutting, my attempt is to mimic that sense of density, complexity, mystery and discovery in the surface of the prairie.

S: That is a beautiful explanation. What does this process teach you about God and about what we humans are doing here? From the simplicity of the surface to the awesome intricacy of the prairie, can you make a connection between prairie-spirit and feeling the presence of God?

Matt: In the Christian spiritual tradition, there is an account of communion with God in the desert like the desert fathers and mothers, which is an aesthetic tradition, but it is also getting out into a landscape that is open and exposed. I think you can get that in the prairie as well as in the desert.

I think back to those large skies and exposed landscapes of my childhood even when the prairie was converted to corn. Being in this kind of empty space or what is perceived to be empty, you are forced to look inward. Your eye doesn't have a place to rest as when we say, "look at that mountain, look at that waterfall, look at that tree." You are not nestled on the prairie—you are exposed, vulnerable.
That can be unsettling.

People who come from the east or west coast often find the prairie unsettling, especially when the wind is blowing. Just the vastness of the space, the emptiness of the space, can force you to ponder your place in the world, in the cosmos and your dependence on the Earth and the Earth's creator.

There is also something about that empty space that connects with, what in the theological tradition is called the Via Negativa. It is understanding God through God's absence or God's silence. The Hebrew Bible also talks about God being manifest in a whisper or in silence.

Or consider Jesus' experience on the cross. According to Jesus' own words, "my God, my God why have you forsaken me?" is a feeling of God's absence. In Christian tradition this is a sense of paradox since God is affirmed to be wholly present in Jesus on the cross. There is a paradox in that sense of emptiness that is part of God's identity. In our experience of vulnerability, of silence in empty spaces, of being alone and experiencing solitude, we can experience a paradoxical presence of God in that absence and emptiness.

S: **There is an almost wordless expansiveness in the prairie. I appreciate the depth of your spiritual connection with your life and work. In your daily life how do you restore that connection? Do you have time to walk or do your artwork alone on the prairie?**

Matt: That question strikes me because lately I feel like I have been missing that. I have my daughter, Lyda, home with me today because she is sick. I have a lot of intersecting projects at the church and school. So, it's been pretty chaotic.

It's important for me to find time to walk in the prairie. In the absence of that, I do get a lot of consolation and rejuvenation from gardening. In the past few years, I have done quite a bit of prairie gardening. I collect native seeds and try to plant my own native plants. Right now in my cellar I have seedlings of purple prairie clover and wild blue indigo. It is an interesting challenge because a lot of these plants are deep-rooted perennials, and they don't invest as much in their seed capacity. It means in the end that it can be difficult to germinate and grow from seed. Some plants can take years before they are ready to bloom. So, it's kind of an interesting activity that takes quite a bit of patience and learning different ways to get the seeds to germinate and then to grow into maturity.

S: **Interesting in that their root system is deep but their seeds are fragile. Their life force seems to be underground, not like corn. Let's talk about when the school building fell into bad disrepair and you and Tia decided to take it on. What was the vision that impelled you to undertake the restoration of the school and the vision that you both hold for it?**

Matt: In terms of people from the outside who took an interest in the school, there were different stages in its history. The Land Institute, a scientific organization out of Salina, Kansas, had a vision for the school. Their primary work is developing perennial grains and developing a form of agriculture they call 'natural systems agriculture,' which is recreating a kind of agriculture that is based on the prairie. They are trying to mimic the resiliency of the prairie's perennial root system. I'm going back to what you are saying about corn versus the prairie.

With the idea of developing a more ecological community, the Land Institute initially bought local properties in Matfield Green and the school back in the 90s. They had successes and failures. They moved out of MG before we moved here, but they had spread some seeds and put down roots here for what might be possible.

A new wave of people came, and they were more interested in art. Ton and Ans are a Dutch couple who moved here and started art galleries. We were involved with the question, what would it be like for MG to be an arts community?

For Tia and I, our interest was not to live in an arts community or to create an enclave of artists in a rural area. We wanted to explore how art and other intellectual pursuits could be integrated into community life and how agricultural rhythms could integrate ecological standards of care. How could these values play a role in building a community? I was interested not so much in a gallery but in having a space that could explore these integrative practices together.

So, here's this building going downhill, not being maintained but once was a multi-faceted space. Four big classrooms, a gym space, grounds around it where we could imagine exploring this more expansive vision of art, agriculture, thinking, celebration and coming together as a community. This felt like the right fit. We needed to find a way of making it work. Eventually, through friends and good fortune, this vision did come to fruition and it is still working.

S: **It is still working! Please tell me why you decided to name it the School for Rural Culture and Creativity?**

Matt: Wendell Berry has talked about culture and its connection to agriculture. The school's website says, quoting from Terry Eagleton too, that "culture" has a root in "agri-culture" that comes from a word meaning "blade of a plow."

Basically, it means the nurturing of natural growth. You can see this if you look at yogurt or cheese. When you look at "cultures", the idea is that you are taking something in nature and nurturing it, you are directing its growth in some way, to serve a human purpose.

When we use the word "culture" in the name of the school, we are uncovering those etymological roots and connecting the idea of culture to rural agrarian life. It has been widely considered that culture is something that happens in the cities. We are taking back some of that initiative.

Also, we are acknowledging that to properly care for the land and sustain large-scale changes that need to happen to live responsibly on the land, things must happen at a cultural level, not just at a policy level.

For people in rural areas, when change happens at a larger scale policy level, it often feels like something is imposed on their communities and that they have little say in the decision-making or power structures.

S: **I know that this effort to develop the school is full of practical issues, but I want to ask the big dream question. What are the big dreams that you and Tia talk about? Even though you might just be the seed spreaders, what do you see that your efforts are cultivating for your children, for future generations?**

Matt: I think eventually we would like to live into the name and the function of the school, into its educational or pedagogical vision. This might mean bringing in interns, doing more workshops and conferences; 'artist in residence' programs where people get to learn artistic techniques like printmaking, or drawing or painting. It might also include learning how to grow your own food, learning how to do canning and preserving, how to identify native plants on the prairie, and learning theology or philosophy. We are trying to develop classroom spaces. The school could offer integral education: a combination of book learning, agricultural knowledge, hands-on work, art activities, collective community projects.

These are the things that we can see in the future. It would require more resources in terms of money and people than we have right now but that is an interesting vision.

S: What I hear you describing is a holistic educational philosophy that brings with it a sense of personal renewal and worth.

Matt: And, where people see their value as human beings, as spiritual beings, as part of the land rather than reducing one's value to economic components that contribute to "the economy."

Sadly, what is happening more and more in the universities is a drive toward careerism, toward a more opportunistic education that is aimed to find you a place in the economy, rather than finding value in yourself.

S: I think it will take leaps of imagination to move priorities from a materialistic world view to values that inextricably connect with nature. How do you experience imagination inspiring you and fueling your work?

Matt: We tend to think of imagination as something to do with fantasy, or like pretend, or something that kids are supposed to have, but imagination is much broader and it is something we can't really live without.

I think we tend to take our sense of reality for granted. That we think this is simply the way things are. But much of our reality is something we have constructed collectively as a society. It involves both our individual imagination and our collective imaginations—the stories that we have told and retold generation after generation—this is what has created and recreated what we call reality now.

Telling stories is something that we are still engaged in. By engaging consciously, we realize that we are interpreters of our reality, that we owe our reality to one another and to the stories that our ancestors have told. This awareness makes us more humble and more perceptive and potentially creative in our engagement with one another and with the earth. We continue to interpret and understand our reality and to find new, more meaningful ways of seeing our place in the world.

S: Last question is about signs of hope. What are signs of hope that your dream for the school is happening?

Matt: I don't know if hope is a metric of something where people tend to look for evidence of this or that change. When we get too caught up in those kinds of evidenced-based metrics, we can lean too far into optimism or despair.

Hope to me is a virtue and even a responsibility. In the Christian tradition, hope begins in a moment of despair when Christ is being executed as a criminal on the cross. Hope can exist in dire circumstances.

I can see it at the level of relationship and the way that people connect to some of the work that we have done and things we've said. During speaker presentations, there has been resonance and not just among people of a particular persuasion. People with seemingly diametrically opposed political beliefs come together when you start talking about things at a more tangible level and when you have built good relationships. We are realizing that conversation and connection are not as impossible as it seems when we are reading the news.

S: I can see the centrality of relationships and creativity in fulfilling your dream. Imagination is key. The emerging life at the School for Rural Culture and Creativity in Matfield Green is a channel of light guiding humanity forward. Thank you, Matt.

To have a place, to live and belong in a place, to live from a place without destroying it, we must imagine it. By imagination we see it illuminated by its own unique character and by our love for it. . . . And it is in affection that we find the possibility of a neighborly, kind, and conserving economy.

— WENDELL BERRY

About Matt

Matt grew up in corn growing fields of central Nebraska. Understanding firsthand 21st-century challenges of rural communities—economic decline, negative stereotyping of rural life, despair and the scarcity of cultural resources, Matt, along with the Matfield Green community, are building up the School for Rural Culture and Creativity. Alongside the hard work of refinishing the floors and installing a new heating system, Matt and the Matfield Green community are building a home-place that cultivates an abiding respect for rural culture, a place of learning where land is cherished, and creative arts thrive. Matt is blurring barriers among intellectual pursuits and varied creative arts—printmaking, writing, gardening, baking pies, telling stories, history, philosophy lectures, scavenging re-useables at rummage sales—all help people and the land thrive together.

Matt is a self-taught printmaker who uses "prairie eyes" to see and appreciate the intricate diversity of prairie plants and grasses. He writes, "the art of landscape is a kind of reciprocal seeing. To represent the place in an image requires faithful observation. So also, the image as an act of interpretation encourages the viewer to return to the place with heightened observation. Any affection inspired by the image is then reflected out again to the place; and, in the affection for place is, as Wendell Berry writes, "the possibility of a neighborly, kind, and conserving economy."

Following Wendell Berry's dictum, "it all turns on affection," Matt's devotion to his family, rural cultural life, right relationship with earth, and faith in a loving, forgiving God is touching the hearts of generations of people past, present and future. Matt serves those who are sustained by the land they call home.

The Ariyaratne Family

If you have a pure heart, if you have a heart that can embrace even the tiniest living being and extend that loving kindness—that is all that matters. To the extent that human beings have expanded to being all embracing human hearts—to that extent we will be developed.

— DR. ARI ARIYARATNE

The Sarvodaya Shramadana Movement

Sarvodaya means the "awakening of all"—from an individual human personality to humanity as a whole. This awakening has spiritual, moral, cultural, social, economic and political dimensions. Whatever we do in one of these sectors influences all the other sectors. Begun in 1953 as an educational experiment to empower people in poor local villages to take responsibility for their wellbeing and livelihoods, Sarvodaya Shramadana has evolved over 70 years into the most progressive and spiritually-rooted community development movement in Sri Lanka.

With a network of 15,000 villages across the country, thousands of staff and villagers work together to identify needs and find ways to make positive change in local communities. Projects involve tangible improvements like building roads and starting preschools, but even more than material results, this integral learning process is rooted in spiritual values aimed to mutually uplift everyone involved. Sarvodaya operates with the motto, "We build the road, and the road builds us."

Having survived decades of civil war, ethnic and religious conflict, economic and political turmoil, corrupt governments, the Sarvodaya movement offers a civic education process that teaches leadership skills and enlists the ingenuity and spiritual values of millions of people to govern for the common good.

Listening to members of the Ariyaratne family (Dr. Ari Ariyaratne, his daughter Dr. Charika Marasinghe and son, Dr. Vinya Ariyaratne) we hear visionary, inner-directed leaders living their values and relentlessly forging a better future for Sri Lanka.

Dr. Ari Ariyaratne

I always share whatever I can. I share my food with a person who is hungry, my knowledge with a person who is ignorant; and I help a person who is sick in any way that I can.

S: Dr. Ari, thank you for speaking with me about humanity's capacity to live from our deepest spiritual values. Your life's work, the Sarvodaya Shramadana Movement, focuses on ordinary people by meeting them with deep respect. How did this life-long commitment begin?

Dr. Ari: I was born in a village of about 1000 families. From this number, about six or seven families were rich and about twenty families were middle class. I belonged to a middle-class family and had the opportunity to go for higher education. Back then, I felt that upper and middle classes ignored the poor. My education was totally in English, but the village children did not have a way to learn English, mathematics or even science. When I saw this, I started evening classes for these children.

Every week I rode my bicycle to school and a poor woman asked me for 25 cents to buy rice. I found that she made ropes out of coconut fiber. For every two rupees that she earned, the middlemen earned about 10 times more. I saw the injustice, not only in education but also in the economic field.

When I was still a schoolboy, I worked in a backward jungle area during vacation. I found a woman with no birthing facilities in her village, so she was by the side of the railway giving birth to her child. Experiences like this made me think that I will educate myself and dedicate my life to serving the poor. Now I am in my 90s, for 77 years since my school days I have been dedicated to serving the poor.

S: The government was after you—the education system didn't like what you were doing. Why were you determined to make the Sarvodaya movement strong?

Dr. Ari: Being a Buddhist, I don't believe that this is my only life. One of the more important things that a Buddhist believes is that this is only one of millions of lives into which one is born and dies. Therefore, focusing on the present life in terms of economics and social development is not

enough. We must think in terms of millions and millions of births and deaths in this cycle. We must know how to put an end to suffering.

What we must do is eliminate whatever greed, whatever anger, whatever ignorance we have in our minds. To do this we have to develop mindfulness. Unlike any other living being we have the capacity to develop mindfulness to the fullest.

So, having been born a human being, I must utilize this human form to attain the highest possible mindfulness. This means that the entire living world is my family. I cannot live without sharing with them. Sharing good conversation, constructive activity and equality should be the principles that guide me in society.

Buddhism gives us principles to follow like sharing, positive speech, constructive action and equality. I always share whatever I can. I share my food with a person who is hungry, my knowledge with a person who is ignorant; and I help a person who is sick in any way that I can.

Our relationships should be based on truth. Never carry false tales, never use harsh language; never use language which is useless. Always speak meaningfully and share pleasant language.

Constructive activity means to abstain from drinking and gambling and from any evil deed we see in society. Equality in association means to treat everybody as a member of your own family. As a human being I should have as my objective total personality awakening. My personality has to awaken—that is, to understand that all living beings are to be respected and never harmed. Never take away life.

To awaken my personality, to live with loving kindness, useful language, constructive activity, there is also equanimity. I should take loss and gain with equal detachment. Buddhist culture gives me these directions to live by.

S: Sarvodaya is translated in different ways. One meaning is, "uplift for the awakening of everyone." Please tell me how you define Sarvodaya?

Dr. Ari: Daya is a Sanskrit word that means awakening. Sarvo means all. The awakening of all is Sarvodaya. Every human being should wish that all human beings awaken. Then only can there be peace and justice in humanity.

S: How does Sarvodaya transfer these values to people?

Dr. Ari: In Sri Lanka, there are about 32,000 communities that are called villages. We plan self-development for individuals, families and for clusters of families that make up a village community.

In Sarvodaya, we have divided 'awakening' to mean: Personality Awakening, Family Awakening, and Community Awakening; and beyond that to National and World Awakening. Those who want to develop their countries should work in these five areas of awakening.

A good human being who believes in building up all humanity is a good national citizen. Those who believe in caste, race and other divisions are doing harm. To help society we need to give up these divisions and come together as humanity.

S: How does Sarvodaya work in the villages?

Dr. Ari: When village people invite me, I go to them and ask what their needs are. They might say, "We need an access road to our village." Sarvodaya volunteers encourage village people to do what they can. Some donate land, others get the needed labor together, some get tools ready while others get meals, etc. With that approach, we can get over 1,000 or 10,000 volunteers and many resources directly from the villages. While there are needs in any community, there are also possibilities and resources.

People can learn self-reliance, not dependence. They can understand how to satisfy their basic needs with their own resources. We, who come from outside, might contribute to specific needs unavailable in the village.

Community development is part of the spiritual, moral and cultural and social awakening of people. Many villages have benefited. Most of all, I have benefited. Because of them I became a better human being.

S: I envision the possibility of a deeper democracy, not what we have now, but people activating democratic governance that is spiritually grounded in compassion, honesty and equity. Do you think that kind of democracy can evolve?

Dr. Ari: To me, democracy is not even a one millionth part of a good life.

S: Tell me more about that.

Dr. Ari: If a society can relate by loving kindness, compassionate action and joy by giving service and equanimity … if human beings can develop these four qualities; and then, if communities can be encouraged to develop self-reliance, participation and an intelligent way of development that includes spiritual, moral and culture aspects, then that is real democracy in action. Democracy is nothing new for people who are awakened. Democracy is a minor part of a total awakening process.

S: Sarvodaya offers a practical model that shows how people can make decisions for their community based on basic values. What gets in the way of spreading this model?

Dr. Ari: You know all over the world people like you and I are trying to release positive forces of democracy in this manner. But remember, all our efforts are nullified by the present political systems. Most of the systems in our country are based on party politics and that ruins all the efforts we make. Seventy years of Sarvodaya's work would have made Sri Lanka much better if not for party politics and for government.

I have never received one cent from the government. Not even a word of encouragement. Despite government systems, we have to do this work. Destroy this present government system, your democracy will succeed. What we must do is … to do what we have been doing but do it better. Let the politicians do their damage and let us do our constructive work.

S: What is your guidance to help people carry on doing what they do, only better?

Dr. Ari: Ultimately all of us, despite the good work we have done, have to die. If you can die in such a way that even better work will continue, that is what matters. Therefore, let us continue to do the good work we have been doing until we die. Let us all get together and build up the human personality that is awakening—that which is always within us. Don't worry about what other people are doing—do what you do right.

S: You said this phrase, "A politician builds culverts, bridges and high-rises, Sarvodaya builds the human heart." What is your hope for building the human heart?

Dr. Ari: If you have a pure heart, if you have a heart that can embrace even the tiniest living being and extend that loving kindness, that is all that matters. To the extent that human beings have expanded to become all embracing, human hearts—to that extent we will be developed. May all the living beings, may all the human beings, may all the other living beings … be happy. That is my wish for all.

While many capitalists and Marxists take spiritual goals to be quietist, mystical, drawing one off into private quests, Sarvodaya's goal and process of awakening pulls one headlong into the "real" world and into the Movement's multi-faceted programs for health, food, education and productive enterprise.

—JOANNA MACY
from her essay
Apostle for Peace

About Dr. ARI

For over seventy years Dr. Ari relentlessly bushwhacked a path through the thicket of politics toward a higher consciousness of community governance. His legacy shows future generations how to integrate secular civic development with spiritual grounding and respect for all life. Dr. Ari passed away one year after this interview, April 16, 2024.

Dr. Ari's belief in rallying ordinary citizens to act from core spiritual principles is carried on by the Sarvodaya Movement and continues to make its mark for the wellbeing of Sri Lanka and for the world.

Dr. Ari has been called the Gandhi of Sri Lanka. A biography of Dr. Ari points out: "Instead of seeing A.T. Ariyaratne like Gandhi or like any other great man and woman of peace, we need to know him as one man who made a difference for millions through Sarvodaya. His message applies to every corner of the Earth where inequity, violence, poverty and hopelessness oppress everyday people struggling to make life worth living."

QUOTED FROM THE *Sarvodaya Newsletter*
"Biography of A.T. Ariyaratne"
DECEMBER 14, 2004

Dr. Vinya Ariyaratne

You cannot save a country [only] by spiritual means, by trying to bring out spiritual values. You need proper governance. There shouldn't be corruption. There should be citizen participation. There should be democracy.

S: I'm glad to learn about Sarvodaya through your eyes and heart. Sarvodaya doesn't use the words "higher education" in the usual sense. How do you understand this term?

Vinya: My father started the Sarvodaya Shramadana movement as an educational experiment when he was a high school teacher. He thought that ten years after independence Sri Lanka needed new directions. He saw that education needed to include personal awakening. Sarvodaya is about an "awakening" which is an educational process that requires attention to inner life, sharing and co-learning.

"Shramadana" means sharing of labor, doing something collectively that will help the community. But in this process, you learn to properly communicate with people, to share and to plan in a systematic way. There is resource management and science behind it.

When Sarvodaya celebrated its 50th anniversary in 2008, we realized it needed to take a bigger step towards transforming society using modern concepts of learning, but with learning that was also deeply rooted in spiritual values.

At that time, we had a campus with basic facilities and held all kinds of training programs: leadership, vocational training, environmental education, community health, enterprise development, youth leadership. We decided that this training needed to be offered not only at the grassroots level, but also to engage policymakers.

The notion of "higher" means to start with an individual at a deeper level. Learning touches your core values. Higher education begins with spiritual development centered in meditation and learning how to interact with other people based on moral, spiritual and cultural values.

So, it is "higher" in that sense, but also "higher" in that it integrates different disciplines and technological skills and builds connections with policymakers. It is about personal transformation through co-learning. It

is experiential learning through engaged, practical interaction with people. That is what we mean by "higher learning."

S: Please give me an example of what this teaching looks like.

Vinya: It is not taught! At Sarvodaya, we just start everything with mindfulness, like we started this call with silence.

In a group, we start by looking at our breathing, in and out. We bring the good energies in the world to heal ourselves and then we transmit this energy to others. We constantly practice bringing in our heart and soul. Rather than telling people what spirituality is, we practice it starting with meditation. Then we engage in activities where we forget about ourselves and try to transform the energy of loving kindness into action.

Villagers need to understand the realities of working in their villages. For example, when you dedicate yourself to the service of others, not everything you do will be received in a positive way. You might be ridiculed and criticized. Then how do you act? In these types of situations, you need to have equanimity that comes from your spiritual level. Unless people are connected spiritually, they can react angrily or stop trying. Sarvodaya helps people use their spirituality to withstand these circumstances. When this is done collectively in a nurturing way, through guidance and mentoring, that is spirituality in practice.

S: Do you find that when people are sharing their own ideas in a group that they tend to help each other more?

Vinya: Yes, exactly. Learning is at two levels; one is at the more intellectual, academic level; the other is, you can't explain it—it is about relationships and energy, which is intangible. At both levels people bond when they see results.

There is a practical and a spiritual element. After villagers cut a road or dig a well, they begin to use the water from the well. Before, they had to travel so long to fetch water, they now feel they have meaning for themselves and in their community. While the source of their inspiration comes from their spirituality, they also see the results of their collective work. People start to believe that the spiritual dimension in life is important. You cannot buy it, you know.

Sustainable development starts with the spiritual element. Of course, people have basic needs to satisfy. They need to have an income. Sarvodaya focuses on social and economic development. Even if villages have economic development based in spiritual moral, social, cultural values, villages also need good governance. That is where political development comes in. Social, economic, government work is inter-related, but the main trigger for effectiveness is spiritual conviction.

S: It is impressive that people are not only meeting in a room meditating, but they meditate and then go out and build a road or make decisions for their village.

Vinya: This comes from Buddhist principles: [Metta] is loving kindness; [Karuna] is compassion, which is transforming loving kindness into action. [Muditha] is the altruistic joy that you get from seeing the results; and [Upekkha] is equanimity where you can face blame, praise, suffering or happiness with a balanced mind.

These are the four principles that awaken a person. The strength of Sarvodaya is that we have been able to introduce these principles in all the communities in our country. One of the key factors for our growth is that people from non-Buddhist traditions accept this philosophy and spirituality.

S: Joy is not usually mentioned when talking about civic responsibility. Please tell me more about this kind of joy.

Vinya: This is a difficult time in Sri Lanka right now. Sarvodaya volunteers care for children who have been abandoned by their parents. When I see the smile on that child's face … I feel joy. When I see hungry people having two meals a day because of Sarvodaya's presence, I feel enormous happiness.

S: Are there stories of civic transformation when people put into practice Sarvodaya's spiritual values?

Vinya: Yes, there are whole communities that became connected at a spiritual level. Following the war here from 1983 to 2009, there was widespread ethnic bigotry and tension. Sarvodaya intervened and tensions diminished. In places where there could have been ethnic riots, communities contained the violence.

While there is a kind of spiritual connection found in every person, the conditions are not always right for people to tap into it. So, what we do is create conditions where this natural human capacity comes out. Of course, there will always be people for whom it does not come out, and that is fine because that is how life works. But most of the time when we create conditions for basic human qualities to come out, they do come out. When people interact and move forward together, it's fantastic!

S: **Sri Lanka has been going through economic distress. Is Sarvodaya's work in the villages making a difference that will endure?**

Vinya: The change is still not deeply rooted. You cannot save a country by only trying to bring out spiritual values.

Sadly, since the war, some Buddhist institutions have issued provocative statements that hinder true Buddhist spirituality. The existing political system has ruined the country and the rule of law. Sri Lanka needs proper governance and government without corruption. It needs democratic citizen participation. Finally, the economic system, not centered on human welfare but on profit generation, has made it difficult for us to find our own way.

We are extremely successful in coming up with economic models based on spiritual values, equity, democracy, participation—but our influence is still not strong enough to cause a political or economic transformation. It's a long journey.

We will continue. We are developing leaders who will take this work forward. I want to dedicate the last part of my life to creating a generation of leaders who can transform our society.

S: **Your daily work must bring you face to face with difficult people and politics. How do you recharge your batteries?**

Vinya: One thing that I have is a strong belief that what we are doing is the right thing. I haven't seen anything better. I think the part that Sarvodaya plays is crucial.

Having said that, when I see the enormous things we face but I don't see institutional and structural change, it's a real frustration. There are times when I feel that we are just cleaning up the mess that somebody has created and continues to create. We try to do certain things outside the normal way, to hold onto democracy in the face of corruption.

Then at the personal level I step back, go to a village or to my office here; this can automatically recharge my batteries. I have tried my best and now I have three younger generations lined up who can take responsibility. I can say, "We may not have succeeded in our lives, but maybe the next generation can fix this." It's not too far, maybe 10 years away.

S: What are your words of wisdom about how to build up the human spirit and help people keep working for change?

Vinya: Dialogue, feeling solidarity, sharing and inspiring each other are so important. I also experience synchronicity—I do things independently but suddenly, unexpectedly I get connected with others and good things happen. It's times like these when I can really feel my heart connected to the work I do.

Soon, I will meet with a group of young people who have planted 120 trees on this campus. We are doing an inventory of how many trees have survived. In my position, I could say, "here's the list, go around and check the trees yourselves." I don't do that. I want to be with them. I feel the importance of that. No matter what high level responsibilities I have I want to go back to my roots. I keep my roots reminded that this is the way forward.

S: You are an inspiration to me. Have a wonderful time looking at the trees with the young people.

The economic system—based on the capitalist model, not centered around human welfare, but on profit generation—has made it very difficult for us to find our own way. We are extremely successful in coming up with economic models based on spiritual values like equity, democracy, participation; but it's still not strong enough to do the final political transformation or economic transformation. It's a long journey.

About Vinya

Dr. Vinya Ariyaratne, Chair of the Sarvodaya Institute of Higher Learning, President of the Sri Lanka Medical Association (2023). Chair of the Sarvodaya Institute of Higher Learning, President of the Sri Lanka Medical Association (2023).

"Just call me Vinya, don't call me doctor" is a request that typifies Vinya's personal warmth and humble ease that come with his vast experience, leadership roles and remarkable accomplishments. The eldest son of Ari Ariyaratne, Vinya was trained as a medical doctor, specialized in public health, and serves as President of the Sri Lanka Medical Association, which he sees as an avenue to impact critical policy change at the national level. Through the years, Vinya served as Executive Director and President of the Sarvodaya Movement, held several appointments in the government as well as the nonprofit public health sector, and is currently the Director of the Sarvodaya Institute for Higher Learning.

In the aftermath of the extended war in Sri Lanka, Vinya developed extensive community health programs that have benefited children suffering the trauma of war; and, he has been involved in civil society peacebuilding and reconciliation initiatives. He keeps a hand in politics and participates in building consensus among key policymakers towards meeting the aspirations of Sri Lankan communities.

Undeterred by achievements and titles, Vinya renews his spirit in his favorite place, his circular office filled with favorite books and big windows that look out on the trees. He cautions himself to go back to his roots, "to keep his roots reminded which is the way forward."

Dr. Charika Marasinghe

I was always bringing in the spiritual dimension. It resonated with my conscience, my mind and heart. This helps me not get stuck in a kind of box. I try to understand how interdependent and interconnected things are and that you can't simply isolate.

S: I'm eager to learn about you. Please tell me about your growing up years in the Ariyaratne family.

Charika: From a young age, spirituality was exposed to us by my parents in a kind of inner, invisible way. We didn't see my father going from Buddhist temple to temple but from day one he exemplified the core principles of engaged Buddhism.

We spent weekends and school holidays in the remotest villages. After school on Friday, my father would ask us to get our mats and pillows and we would drive to a remote village about five or six hours away. When I was about sixteen, we had traveled through every nook and corner of the country.

Our family didn't have a house of our own. We lived in a small space at the Sarvodaya headquarters. My father wanted us to be part of a larger community rather than being isolated in a family setting cut off from the rest of the world. Who I am today has a lot to do with that community way of upbringing.

Our parents wanted us to see suffering firsthand. During our visits to villages, when the elders went for discussion, we went looking for children to play with. In one village we found children who didn't have proper clothes to wear. When I was eight years old, my brother Vinya and I wrote an article asking people to help these children and we sent it to a newspaper. We received so many clothes and books in response! This action gave birth to Sarvodaya Children's Groups that helped needy children for many years. My early beginning working for child rights helped forge my path as a lawyer for children's rights and human rights.

In 1979, the International Year of the Child, Sarvodaya was invited to implement a children's exchange program between Sri Lanka and the

Netherlands, and I was asked to select the children. I felt that if we were to do justice for Sri Lankan children, then I should go to the Sarvodaya villages and interview 50-60 children and then select the best so the children could feel that each one was selected on their own merit and that it was a fair process. We selected wonderful children from the Sinhala, Tamil, Hindu, Muslim and Christian traditions.

In the Netherlands they were like stars! They were so wise in their responses to questions by Dutch National Television. They were asked, "What do you think about the skyscrapers?" The children answered, "even though you have huge high-rise buildings and big highways...we have the cool breeze that we experience in our villages...we don't think you enjoy the happiness in your big cities that we experience in our humble villages."

An interviewer asked a child, "Why did your country become poor, and our country become rich?" A boy from one of the poorest areas in the Northern provinces said, "You, the Dutch colonial masters, came to our country, took our wealth and you all became rich, and we all became poor." The interviewer answered, "Yes, we are trying to repay the damage that we caused to your country." These kinds of encounters happened.

When we moved into our own house and I had some space, I felt I needed to focus on education because as a woman it would give me the power and voice to contribute to my society.

I was clear that I wanted to work in human rights law. I learned that Sarvodaya lawyers in the North Central Province were helping poor farmers get farming land. Some of us learned this area of law and started the Sarvodaya Legal Services Movement at the national level. In 25 years, it became the largest legal services project in the country with about 100 volunteer lawyers.

During the insurrection by the Sinhala Marxist group, I typed letters as an 11-year old child at the Sarvodaya office. I had to put a pillow on the chair because I wasn't tall enough to reach the typewriter. Six years after the 1971 insurrection when several thousand youth were killed and insurgents took over police stations, 49 leaders were arrested and kept in a Colombo prison. During this time, the Prime Minister who was the first woman Prime Minister in that position, invited Sarvodaya to rehabilitate those prisoners.

When my father learned about the predicament of this incarcerated youth, he realized that these youths were intelligent, so he set up a small library inside the jail. By studying inside the prison several youths sat for the university entrance exam and entered university. I witnessed how Sarvodaya was putting kindness into action and trying to rehabilitate. After his release from prison the insurrectionist leader came straight to my father to express his gratitude.

Sarvodaya helped me bring a holistic perspective to look at social and political issues and structures. In 2007, I was given the assignment to develop a five-year strategic plan to fight against bribery and corruption for Transparency International Sri Lanka. A foreign consultant and I worked together. After the strategic planning exercise, the consultant told me that although it was strategic work we did, he felt it was also a spiritual exercise. He gave me a book by Peter Senge from the US and told me, "What you are doing is what Peter Senge is teaching at MIT." I read Peter Senge's books and wanted to study with him, but it was beyond my means to go to MIT.

I was always bringing in the spiritual dimension. It resonated with my conscience, my mind and heart. I think this gives me a different perspective. It feels very valuable and helps me not get stuck in a kind of box. I try to understand how interdependent and interconnected things are. You simply can't isolate.

I noticed how my father took risks. Usually, when people attempt to undertake something, they plan and consider the pros and cons. My father would follow his intuition. If in his heart he felt that this is what the country needed, he would go ahead. Then, he would look for people to fund it and do the work.

Always, he had a dream and he felt it could be achieved. He had so many dreams, I feel like I too have these dreams. My parents would not give lectures on how we should be spiritually. They gave us freedom to dream and to forge our own paths.

There was one exception. When I got the highest scores in my university entrance exam, my father said, "Don't go to the university, work for Sarvodaya." I told him, "Father, you have six children, at least allow one child to work outside of the Sarvodaya structure. I will carry the Sarvodaya values in my heart."

He was not happy. But I was determined to find my own path. Also, I changed my name after I got married because I really did not want to be under the Ariyaratne shadow. I wanted to find the path that was coming from inside of me. Doing things under my own name has always been important. I have largely succeeded in forging my own identity apart from the Sarvodaya and the Ariyaratne name.

S: Your spiritual conviction carried you through your studies and work. How do you ground yourself and enrich your spirit?

Charika: On a daily basis, I try to find time for myself. I felt that my parents never did that. When they were trying to build a movement, they had to make selfless sacrifices, and this took its toll on their health. Their mental health was good because they were rejoicing and translating their work into compassion, but they neglected to take care of their physical health. When I reached 40, I realized that if I didn't care for myself, I would end up with all kinds of health issues later.

Also, I've seen human rights lawyers getting cancer. Early on, I felt that I didn't want to be an adversarial lawyer because I cannot change my way of interacting with people. In a court of law, you can't be you. I didn't want to pretend to be someone else in a court of law! I followed a non-adversarial way of approaching human rights. It was difficult to follow my spiritual path and at the same time be adversarial. I still haven't learned the art of approaching human rights in an adversarial way while keeping my spiritual core intact.

In my human rights and women's rights work I saw so much anger and so much attrition. I saw people falling ill and leaving this world at a very young age.

When I was teaching International Law and the Philosophy of Law, I used to tell students that people don't come to a lawyer if they are happy. They come if they are suffering and cannot resolve an issue on their own. Both lawyers and doctors meet human suffering firsthand.

I meet victims of abuse as well as the perpetrators of abuse and violence. Perpetrators have so much despair. They have so much anger and a sense that they have suffered injustice, so they feel that it is ok to get revenge from the one who did them harm.

S: When you are engaging in your work how do you keep spiritually centered and balanced?

Charika: Actually, my graduate studies at Oxford put me on a more personal spiritual path because I had to keep myself reminded that there is more to life. To me, Oxford was an artificial, academic environment. During the day I read all kinds of law reports and documents about human rights. I decided that on a daily basis I needed to attend to my own spirituality, so I registered in an Oxford Buddhist Society and started reading a book by Thich Nhat Hanh each night before going to bed. I've always wanted to learn the spirit behind something for myself, not just because someone was asking me to do something. My father always said, "be a vegetarian." But it was only one fine day that I made the decision for myself.

It has always been my dilemma to weigh everything in terms of spiritual values. That's not easy. About two years ago, an international organization invited me to get involved in a huge child abuse investigation. I accepted on the condition that we agree on clear due process and principles. It involved a very attractive monetary package and for three months I worked, helping with the investigation. I felt it was so important for children and that my expertise could be used to address issues that would impact children in about 20 countries. It was in that spirit that I accepted the job.

But then I realized the process was not democratic, right? At that point, I decided that I didn't want to tarnish my integrity because I value my integrity more than my life. I wrote to the President of the organization and said that I have a strong moral conscience from my family upbringing and that my two Oxford law degrees in human rights and child rights had given me a strong sense of justice. He asked if I was stepping down because the monetary package was not attractive. I said that it had nothing to do with that. Basically, I have not allowed any international agency, a UN agency … or an NGO to buy me for what they want to communicate to the world.

Spirituality is my own introspective awareness in solitude as well as in my professional life. I can't separate the two. My solitude practice gives me the clarity of mind and the openness of heart to decide and weigh what is best for my clients and the people I serve.

S: In your poem, "Supreme Liberation"—you write that your own integrity is to look inside yourself and ask, "Is this how I want to live?" You say that this is a personal way of seeding a revolution of personal integrity.

Charika: Of course, this attitude is not financially advantageous. But I would rather live this way and preserve my own sanity. The challenge has been how to integrate my spiritual and moral values when dealing with people and political systems that have strayed so far from their values and the mission.

One example was during COVID when I was asked to head The Law Reform Committee. I felt that they were trying to destroy the wholesome cultural and spiritual practices relating to family life in Sri Lanka. They were trying to make very liberal changes to the system without taking note of the wholesome cultural and spiritual ways that nurture parent-child relationships. The chairperson and I were in the minority view and both of us stepped down.

S: **Your vision for humanity may happen in the future if humanity evolves in that direction. Do you have hope in where humanity is going?**

Charika: My hope is like swimming upstream. I think most of the countries in the world have lost their independence, lost their freedom— not just to the most powerful economic and political blocks in the world, but also to regional political structures and powers.

I visited the European Union website, where you find the tagline "Promoting European Values." In Sri Lanka, we don't want European money that is given to promote European values. We have a rich wholesome system of values in this part of the world in the East.

The challenge for future leaders is how to balance economic freedom with whatever spiritual and moral values they are trying to promote. If you lose economic integrity, you cannot preserve and retain space for the spiritual.

There is hope only if everyone takes their own understanding, finds their own role in this complex governance system. This is when change can really happen. Because the system is failing, right? It is crashing. It is a matter of time.

The challenge is that in Sri Lanka we need resources. Projects here are being driven by the donors' agendas. It used to be that they allowed the organization the freedom to decide what was best for the country. Now donors come with their own global and regional agendas and don't give space for local organizations to forge their own strategies. To effect change the local people need to be part of a collective process. The question is to what extent local groups can be self-reliant.

S: **Your story from Ward 8 in the hospital reflects cultural values that reside within people. What values did you witness there?**

Charika: When you belong to a low-income group, you cannot survive unless every family member supports one other. When you are economically powerful, you don't need family support. In our country, where we are suffering with all kinds of issues—cost of living, lack of electricity, our cultural values have kept people intact. When someone gets sick, relatives apply for leave from work to take care of them. That family spirit is still intact. But if tragedy happened to someone in the middle income or upper middle income, now they might be told, "We need our privacy. Don't come. We want to relax and recuperate." In the low-income groups, it is human interaction. It is the coming together that shows we truly care for each other and that is so powerful.

In Ward 8 I saw how attached the children were to their parents and how attached siblings were to each other. In our part of the world, a child is looked after by so many generations, not just the mother and father.

Will these practices be taken to the next generation? We don't know. Children and young adults are bombarded with so much information. I don't know to what extent they will be able to balance the modern world and these cultural, spiritual values. My nieces and nephews were exposed to a Western education at a young age and influenced by a Western kind of thinking. Whether or not they are going to take our value system beyond their generation, I don't know.

We try to inculcate cultural values within a family system, assuming the children—when stepping out of the home into the larger world—will carry those values. It depends on how powerful the materialistic forces are coming from outside. These are difficult choices. It's a dilemma every country must face. If we are to see a positive change, influence must happen at the individual family, school and community level. We need to create structures at those levels to keep cultural values intact.

S: **Your intelligence is sharp, and your spiritual insight is the same.**

Charika: I draw inspiration from the late monastics, enlightened women who had to go through so much. We are part of a bigger cycle. We are reaping the positive and negative things that previous generations have sown. We can create causes and conditions now for future generations. We may not be alive to see the results, but at least we have emanated something positive to the universe. Humanity is awakening to a new reality. A revolution of consciousness is in the making. Be a whole-hearted participant in this revolution.

About Charika

Charika is an internationally respected human rights and child rights lawyer, professor of law and policymaker. A life-long activist striving for justice and as a legal professional working within traditional economic and government structures, Charika advocates for radical change. She calls forth a new generation of "social architects" who can reshape cultures by replacing the power of politics and greedy acquisitiveness with the power of personal mindfulness, selfless giving, interdependence and cooperation.

As a trustee of the Vishva Niketan International Peace and Meditation Center in Sri Lanka (the spiritual arm of Sarvodaya), Charika creates programs that provide psycho-social and spiritual support to prisoners, trauma victims, and thousands of ordinary volunteers and villagers in the Sarvodaya Movement.

Charika says that she must have heard the word "awakening" in her mother's womb. Inspired by her parents, the Sarvodaya Movement and the teachings of Buddhist philosopher Joanna Macy, Charika believes that a "revolution of consciousness is in the making." In Charika's poem "The Great Turning," she urges people to participate in this revolution by shifting priorities …

From selfish accumulation to selfless giving, from industry-based to sustainability-based societies, from supermarkets to village market, from urban development to rural development, from dominance and separation to peaceful coexistence, from business to beauty of sacred silence, from isolation and dependence to interdependence and interconnectedness of all life.

The Great Turning
— CHARIKA MARASINGHE

James Offuh

Let's go. If we do not go meet with the warring groups who will go? I asked myself a question: What have I achieved in life that is a sign of courage? Yes, I have a family, but we don't live only for our family, we live for others. I said I must go!

His barbershop doubles as a community meeting place.

James Offuh's divine calling to be a peacemaker beams through his eyes and big smile with disarming clarity and light. He credits much of his bright optimism and his knowledge of conflict mediation to his mentors Len and Libby Traubman. From them, he learned how to convey to people that they have value and that you care about them and love them. His barbershop doubles as a community meeting place, a conflict management school, a children's library, and an online international peace center. Offuh and his wife Ola say they realized the value of peacemaking in their marriage when they started learning about one another not only as husband and wife, but as human beings.

"Barbering" hair, providing a safe place, asking to hear people's stories, listening and letting people know they matter is transforming lives as well as changing laws in West Africa. Offuh and Ola rely on their faith and their resourcefulness to build up their family, their country and the world.

S: So good to speak with you, Offuh. In a prior conversation you told me that you are living in accord with your divine purpose. How did you come to this understanding and commitment?

Offuh: My journey personally has been divinely oriented. When it comes to my peace mission I see it as a calling, a vocation. I see it my as divine responsibility given to me to help save the world.

In 2012, I was meditating early in the morning in my barbershop when I heard the news that people were being slaughtered in Cote D'Ivoire. There was fear everywhere. All we heard was news of death, calamity and uncertainty. There was internal displacement of people from different regions. Pregnant women and children were in terrible hardship after so much human slaughter.

Every business was closed down because of the war. My barbershop remained open because people needed services for their hair. They had to stay indoors because of fear of bullets and the war, but their hair kept growing so the barbershop became a gathering center. Every ethnicity—all kinds of people would come to have their hair cut. That is where my peace journey began.

I asked myself the question: "Why must violence be used as a way for seeking social, political change? Why must it be war that brings change? Why must killing be the chosen option? Why not talk? Why not talk?" At that moment I did not know what dialogue meant. I did not have a good understanding of what peacemaking or conflict resolution dialogue meant.

I felt the yearning of my soul as a result of this catastrophic situation. We were all exposed to the same situation—no one was exempt. It became the talk of the day. My customers spoke of the violence and everyone was afraid. We were experiencing bullets flying past our homes at night: It was chaotic. As I was barbering them, we would talk about the situation that was so challenging for everyone.

Because of the war, people were experiencing isolation. They didn't have the freedom to go outside to socialize. My barbershop became the place where people could easily come since there was no other activity in town. Even after I finished barbering people they did not leave. That is how I discovered that people were getting more interested in talking about the problems.

I asked my "second" to take over my barbering position while I continued the conversations. There was no space inside my shop where people could sit in a large circle, but there was a bench outside where people were sitting. Having conversations with people took up much of my time. People would come to have their hair barbed and I would say, "Who wants to talk about the situation and possible solutions and who wants to barb their hair?" That was how I started forming a community around the question: "What is possible to champion the idea of peace in the midst of violence?" That was how I started this journey.

S: **What encouraged the people to speak up and to feel safe with you in those first conversations?**

Offuh: They sensed that my heart was authentic, that I was so troubled about the situation and that I wanted to bring solutions. Talking with people from a grassroots perspective about their ideas for resolving the conflict became very interesting.

At that time, I didn't have education or training in social dialogue or peacemaking. What I had was the authenticity of my heart, my listening and creating a circle of hope that allowed people to come together and socialize. They said, "Now we can come out and be with each other." We created a socializing space where we told stories and shared experiences about what was going on. Conversations kept building. What did I do? Because of the stories that people were sharing, we started to find common values about what we wanted and what might be possible ways to prevent such a situation from happening in the future.

More people kept coming. We could see people coming from the government ministry, journalists, lawyers, teachers, parents and people in different leadership roles. I discovered that people coming together from different institutions and organizations was a community asset. They came to have their hair cut but their conversations turned into important community interactions. Conversations kept building. That was it!

S: **You were learning dialogue process just by doing it. When did you decide to get training and become a peacebuilding educator?**

Offuh: In 2008, I applied to join a Peace Studies and Conflict Resolution course with an online university in Nigeria. They gave me a provisional admission, but I couldn't go because the fee was high. I am the father of four kids, and I had to take care of them. But I didn't stop, I kept asking how do I acquire knowledge and peacemaking skills through the internet?

I started visiting cyber cafés and I searched Google for terms like making peace, conflict transformation, dialogue, etc. I got replies and information back and printed out as many as possible and kept learning on my own.

I wrote to an organization in London about my vision for peace in my country and about what peace means. I wrote how I feel about peace and what I wanted to do. They contacted me a few weeks later and we started interacting. That is what led to my meeting Len and Libby Traubman. When Len and Libby read my philosophy and theology about peace, they became interested in my thinking and my heart's curiosity about what peace means. We started relating. They sent me a video of a peacebuilding conference they led called "Dialogue in Nigeria." We dove into what dialogue means and I started learning from that step forward.

S: I know you deeply respect Len and Libby. Of all the things you received learning from them, what were the most important gifts? How did they help you learn to be a peacebuilder?

Offuh: They were the most wonderful, compassionate mentors that I would ever have. Through their work "Living Room Dialogues" which they started in their home, they were involved with Jewish Palestinian issues. They developed a one-to-one conflict resolution method that serves as a global model for educators, activists, researchers, journalists and strategists, including me. Len offered idealism and compassionate mentorship rooted in his love for humanity. He taught me that sustained listening and effective communication are fundamental for repairing human relationships.

That idealism was a virtue that Len passed on to me. Taken from a philosophical standpoint, Len's idealism became a way of seeing reality. The idealism that Len taught me conveyed that All is One. The sense that All is One really gave me confidence and the skill to synergize differences among people.

S: You come into a conflict situation with a preconceived affirmation in the ideal that All is One. You trust people can move into this ideal reality and begin to see their similarities and how they connect. Underneath conflict the reality is that All is One. Is that right?

Offuh: Yes, exactly. What is conflict? Literally, conflict is when there is an end of understanding. Misunderstanding happens when people's individual lens of seeing things takes over and there is no good way to communicate. There will always be a gap when individuals don't have sustained dialogue skills or conscious listening skills. With these skills people can observe, understand and use different mental models that synthesize different ways of thinking for the good of all. The miracle is that we can close the gaps that lead to conflict by deep listening and communication skills, which humanize and dignify a person.

S: **Please tell me a story where you applied that kind of conscious listening. You've been involved in major social conflicts in Cote D'Ivoire. Can you share a story about a situation when these skills made a difference?**

Offuh: Yes, I can speak on a personal and professional level. As a family man, a husband and a father, I discovered that parenting with love is like listening with love. When you listen with love, you don't stigmatize, you don't judge. You are open, mindful and you empathize by embracing the value and the principles of the other. Everyone has a value. People's lenses (how people see things) and their mental models are shaped by gender, culture and religion. These dimensions shape how people see life, reality and it influences their perspectives.

On the personal level, I listen very deeply to my wife. That helps our marriage to be sweeter and more sustained over time. Also, my children become part of the conversation because I show them that their opinions matter. I show them that what they say can shift the paradigm. The inclusiveness that enters our family by honoring everyone's voice and each person's values make relationships in my home and my family very sweet.

On a professional level, I mitigated conflict in a post-tribal war situation in Cote D'Ivoire. In 2014, there were massacres between two tribes that arose from a land dispute and no solution came from the legal system.

I wanted to invite the two tribes into dialogue. The fear was that these people would fight again if they came together to dialogue. My team said they would not go because that area was marked as a red zone where no one should go. I said, "Let's go. If we do not go, who will go?" I asked myself a question: what have I achieved in life that is a sign of courage? Yes, I have a family, but we don't live only for our family, we live for others. I said, "I have to go!" God told me he was waiting for me out there.

That is how my faith strengthened my peacebuilding. We used listening skills to guide the dialogue process. And it worked! I believe that "An enemy is someone whose story you have not heard." People judge the other because they fear the other. They fear the other because they are ignorant of the other. This approach really works!

S: **You are a man of deep faith. How does your faith guide, inspire and renew you? How does your faith show up in this work?**

Offuh: When you discover purpose, your heart receives that purpose as your responsibility. Something pulls you to venture into that purpose and get it done. It all started in the barbershop even without prior training! At five in the morning on April 1 I was doing my meditation at my barbershop. I was singing a spiritual song of devotion to God, a small voice said to me, "unite communities for peace." Then the voice said, "to save humanity from destruction."

"Unite communities for peace to save humanity from destruction." When I heard those two phrases together, I said, "God, I have no knowledge, no skills in peacemaking. Why do I have to do this?" And I heard a voice clearly answer, "I am the Prince of Peace. I will teach all you need to know. Wise men from the East will come and teach you all you need to know." That voice took me to the Book of Isaiah 58:12.

> *For they that shall be of me shall build up the old waste places;*
> *I shall raise up the foundations of many generations; and, I shall be*
> *called the Repairer of the breach, the Restorer of the part to dwell in.*

After that, Libby and Len Traubman came into my life. It was very clear. I discovered that the validation of my mandate was clearly described in this passage. Since then, I have experienced divine visitations.
When you look at the logo of my organization, you will see hands and a dove. God said, "In my hands is the peace that I offer to humanity." The dove was the symbol of that.

I had a dream, and in that dream, I heard a voice say, "Look up at the sky." And I looked up in the sky and I saw a white dove. And that voice said, "Raise your right hand up." When I raised my hand up, that dove rested on my right hand. When I woke up, I looked up the symbolic meanings for a dove. I said this is my new identity. This is what I am called to do. Since then, my peacebuilding work has continued.

Before I went to the post-war tribal negotiation, in a dream I heard a voice. A man came to me and said, "Before you go on that journey you need to be empowered because you go alone." Then he brought a bowl and poured honey into it; and again, he poured olive oil into that bowl and then mixed them. He asked me to kneel, and he poured the oil on my head. When I woke up, I understood the journey was safe. From then until today, the peace missions have not failed.

S: That story affirms that God, a Higher Power, is there to protect our efforts, to be a companion in our lives. Therein lies hope that human beings can live in alignment with a divine connection. How do you pass on this possibility to others?

Offuh: The greatest joy for someone like me is to share the courage I receive from these "voices" with someone who is doing the same work. The only way to institutionalize a concept is to pass it on to people who receive it with the same poignancy and vigor and continue the journey.

Before I came to the U.S. God spoke to me. He said, "Your visit to the U.S. is a visit between Elijah and Elisha. When you go, and you return, your mentors will go to rest." I didn't understand what that meant. When I came to the United States, Len took me as his own mentor, and he gave me a staff as a symbol of creative initiative.

Len told me that in his 35 years of experience he had not seen anyone interpret his "Dialogue for Peace Model" the way I had. Len said that he was ready to pass his mantle to me. He said, "Okay, James, now you do that." It was not long after that meeting that Len unexpectedly got sick and passed away. I think this was spiritual transference.

Mentorship for me is like parenting. What I call parenting with love is mentoring with compassion. When you mentor with compassion, you are mindful and empathic. You listen deeply to the other and share your heart. People connect to that energy, and they grow.

S: You understand mentorship as a way to invite others to find their own purpose and access to divine inspiration. That brings us to a bigger question. You said that you are here to "save humanity from destruction." Is that possible?

Offuh: From my experience, trust is missing in our culture. So many things have become a danger to trust building: politics, religion, culture, education, classism. All these things are a threat to building trust.

The only way for humanity to connect to an ideal reality of our Oneness is through education. Experience has taught me that there are some things that only governments can do, such as negotiate peace agreements. There are things that citizens can do such as transform conflictual human relationships, modify human behavior, change social political culture. The capacities and energies of citizens are the world's greatest untapped resource in meeting the challenges of the 21st century.

Effective democracy and social economic development depend on building effective human relationships. Good relationships are only possible through sustained dialogue, being open to one another. We can do this by embracing the beauty of diversity and uncovering a new social intelligence that reveals a vision of a future world that works for everyone.

S: **Effective democracy seems unreachable now, but when you break it down to listening and valuing differences in people, anybody can do it. You also had a vision to open a peace library for children at your barbershop. Is that happening?**

Offuh: The library is a response to the people. Before we had the library, children were on the streets. Parents and schools lacked tools for educating children in a deeper way. I am not talking about teaching mathematics or geography. I am talking about teaching those transformative values that connect hearts and minds and spirits with others. I'm talking about woman-centered values—how to love, how to respect, how to value the other. The library is stirring up the desire for love to become our culture.

If we want the next generation to become authentic leaders, we have to show them the way to become passionate readers. It is really inspiring to me that the kids choose the library versus going to game stations. They come to the library at any time. They can spend 5 minutes, 30 minutes or any time they feel like. The purpose is to encourage kids to learn, to love and to embrace books as a toy.

S: **You are answering a question I had about building up the human heart. How can we continue to help each other build up our hearts so that we build a culture of more trust and love?**

Offuh: I think it's an educational approach, a skill transfer. That is why educators are needed. Parents and leaders in all sectors need to learn about the principles and practices of global citizenship education, transformative education, so that they know how to work with the differences we see in the world. We all are different, that is the reality. Learning to live respectfully with differences in human beings should be the main focus.

There will be conflict and mishandling of conflict, violence in families, in communities, in corporations and in countries if people are not trained to synergize their differences as a competence for human and community development. We need to synergize differences to have success in the human experience. Without this change, our world will always suffer the triple evil that Dr. Martin Luther King spoke about: militarism, poverty, racism. These will be used as weapons against others to control the differences.

When education closes the gaps, we will discover a new social intelligence. We will experience new creativity and enter a new paradigm that will preserve a world where we will begin to see peace and justice in human existence.

S: You are saying competence in these principles and practices need to grow worldwide and you sound determined. I am so glad you are a peace educator. Is there anything else you'd like to say before we close our time together?

Offuh: Transforming violence to peace, domination to interconnectedness, will only be possible when the imagination of people at the grassroots moves them to see themselves as peacebuilders and to take responsibility for their communities. This is a tangible possibility for me. A world of peace with nonviolence and justice in all forms is possible. I think the biggest threat to human security and development is people not taking responsibility for change. We must begin with ourselves. A transformative shift in us that impacts interpersonal relationships will ripple out to form collective efforts for community development. System-thinking focus will address the status quo of militarism, poverty and racism. Your choice makes a difference.

About Offuh

James Offuh resides with his family in Abidjan, Cote D'Ivoire. He is a passionate peace advocate, relationship builder, civic educator, communication skills facilitator and a barber. He practices an inclusive universal Christian faith. James is President/Founder of an NGO-UFPACI, United for Peace Against Conflicts International.

One of the most significant achievements of UFPACI was the successful reconciliation of two tribes, entrenched in violent rivalry—the Gueres and Dozos. He has reconciled albinos and non-albinos and Christians and Muslims and has worked to integrate people with handicaps into society. He is a local and international peace educator and serves as a mentor for peacebuilders from all over the world who want to learn from him.

Offuh believes that everyone has a compassionate spirit, even those who seem to be terrorists. He calls for the need to give space for their spirit to come forward and the humanity in them to be revealed.

Jon Rasmussen

What do I have to give in my life? My three-word answer, "I love people."

Self-described as "somewhat of a rascal" who likes to stir things up a bit, at professional conferences Jon creates spaces for people to move from behind their speaker-podiums to get to know one another as human beings. After a brush with his own death and a diagnosis of a serious chronic disease, Jon pressed reset and asked himself, "what do I have to give in my life?" His three-word answer, "I love people," became the portal for a career focusing on dialogue facilitation, mediation, International Scout leadership; and, by just showing up, making people feel truly welcomed for who they are.

Jon naturally makes the journey from his head to his heart when he creates safe space for deeper conversations and develops innovative educational projects so young adults can follow through on their own initiatives. He has been called many things: peace builder, educator, dialogue facilitator, problem solver, organizational leader. Jon says that one thing is certain—he aims to light a flame in people's hearts and minds that fires them up to see a need and step into the action to make a positive difference.

S: When we first met on Zoom, I was touched by your quality of gentleness that felt loving and affirming. I would love to know the events or markers in your life that helped you become the person you are.

Jon: That's a difficult question in a way. I've always been a learner in life. I've never really focused on things to achieve but just to have a meaningful and good life.

All my learning has come retrospectively. "Ok, that happened and that's why that happened." I think my main way of being human comes fundamentally from my parents and my grandparents.

My entire upbringing has been very open and has included values of being helpful to other people, of being there and always being as good as the human being you are. I think there is a kind of fundamental love that has been flowing from family my whole life. I never realized it until I became older and said, "Oh, God that is why I am doing all these things." I have experienced this love my whole life through my parents and grandparents. I didn't see it before, but it has been with me unconsciously. There have been moments of realizing that things needed to change for me to be the person that I am today.

Thirty years ago, I was enrolled in a military leadership academy. I was diagnosed with Crohn's disease, and they didn't allow me to continue. I was out the door. I said to myself, "Ok … now what?"

I have the ability to rebuild old vintage cars and I worked with that for 15 years. But my health got worse and worse. In 1999 I had to undergo surgery and almost lost my life. After that, I was barely anything of my former self.

I am a creative person. I love to rebuild things, paint and do sculpture. But even doing all those things my health got worse and worse until I had to stop and rethink my life. I had to ask myself, "What do I have?" I have myself at least. I started to look at my other qualities. Besides creativity, my focus has always been on humans. Humans have always been a major focus for me—taking care of other people, talking with people. I have a very easy connection with people. That was my main topic in school. During free time, I went out to talk with the other kids. I could be friends with anybody. It was so easy for me.

I still have Crohn's, there is no cure. But the path I'm on today opens me to the spiritual dimension of life. I am trying to make deeper connections with people. My health has been without complications for 30 years. My medication works and it's just really nice.

S: **I'm sorry you took a dive with Crohn's disease, but you used it to ask yourself the best question. What fulfills your heart? Experiencing your ease with people, what have you learned about making these deeper connections with people?**

Jon: I think I have some kind of … (I'm rephrasing it in my mind … I always forget what to say) … but I have a way of understanding people. Some call it intuition. I don't know what it is, but I have a good way of connecting with people and sensing how they are doing. I can easily spot if a person is feeling insecure, unsafe, in a good mood or whatever. I somehow spot people who could use a shoulder to rest against. There is some other kind of connection beyond just the listening and the verbal part. I have a spiritual dimension with people, it is a connection with—it's difficult to say in words.

S: **I'm curious about how you make a deeper connection with people?**

Jon: Hmmm. I like to connect, and I like to have that focus. It comes gently and without complications. I can easily connect with anybody, and I rarely have conflicts with people. When people have conflicts with each other, I can easily connect with both sides. I don't know how to put it. I have stepped into many conflict situations between people and somehow it seems that people want to hear what I have to say rather than moving on with the conflict.

S: **What is it about you that gives people a sense of trust and safety?**

Jon: That's the strange part … I am asking myself that question all the time too. What is it that people sense in me? Even with you, you said that you felt some kind of presence in me that you found interesting to explore.

In my mind, I'm still a five-year-old, very shy boy … but even so I have a connection talking to people. I can go on public transport, and someone will always come and talk to me. Ok, so I am just standing there, and I wonder what about me looks welcoming to you. It's one of those things that I have difficulty figuring out. I know that I am a very calm person. I also show that I want to listen to people. I want to know who you are.

People fascinate me and I have an interest in knowing why people are the way they are.

S: I think that is the key, Jon. You have an openness and a sincere curiosity so that the person feels given to, not taken from. It's interesting that this is an intuitive, energetic connection rather than a set of skills.

Tell me about your spiritual life. Is there a God in your world?

Jon: Ohhh … so, we are Lutheran Protestants. The church for us is free and open, we can pick and choose. We don't go to church every Sunday, but I do feel a strong connection to it and I would never abandon it. There is more to it than what I was brought up to believe. Society is structured in such a way that religion has become more like a culture.

I do feel a strong presence in it … somehow … somehow? I don't feel a daily connection, but I go to church and to the cemetery from time to time. I just like just being there. Of course, I like the songs, but I couldn't quote anything from the Bible.

I think there is a sense of spirituality that has no name. Just like so many facets in my life, I can't put a name or a label on it, it is just there, and it is always nonjudgmental. My approach to people or religions is just what I see is what I get rather than what other people have told me is the truth.

S: People are yearning for more of this kind of spirituality but it's still hard to put into words. I've been afraid to match the word, 'spiritual' with 'democracy.'. It doesn't feel right—yet. I look for the deeper spirit that comes through people as they take on leadership.

Jon: True, true. There are so many unconscious things. Let's say that what I love about my church is that the priest is like me. He is a normal person walking his dog and focusing on things that reflect the everyday life that I relate to. I know he has to quote certain things from the Bible, but it's always with a sense of humor and with a sense that this is about the life that you are going to live when you go out the door.

S: The connection with your priest is about you both being human together. It sounds like you get the sense of who you are reinforced in your church experience.

Jon: Yes, there will always be something for me in this experience. Absolutely.

About this interconnectedness—like what you said you noticed in me. There is something in my presence to be explored. There is something in my voice that is calming and conveys a big level of trust. There is some kind of trust present without me saying it. I don't understand it but I'm glad that I have a long life and that I still have things to discover.

S: I like it that you are a bit unconscious about what it's about. If you knew the answers or took this trait for granted, that attitude would undermine the beauty of this gift.

Let's talk about the work you are doing now. You wear different hats but let's start with the World Organization of Scouts Movement because I know that it is a huge passion of yours. How do you see the impact of your leadership?

Jon. It's a family thing. My parents and grandparents were scouts as kids, but I was not. I was a 70s child and was just asked what I wanted to do. I just did what my friends did. But we had those scout values in my family, and they have always been part of my life.

Things I do in scouting, I do because there are present and future generations of kids who I feel need to have the best opportunities to be who they are and to make the kind of world that they want to have. If I can contribute in any way to boost programs and teach values that will improve their chances to succeed in life, then my work is successful. It's all for them—it's for the young people.

S: Give me an example of an important value that you continue to pump into the organization and that you want the scouts to receive.

Jon: Recent things I have been working on sound so boring—but it is education. It focuses on intercultural and interreligious dialogue and how to understand your life in a more positive way. I want people to know who they are so they can understand how other people are. Then they can open doors and communicate with each other.

To have positive dialogue with each other is what I have been working on for the last six years. I've been giving training to adults and kids and continuously improving the program to focus on the on-the-ground things kids can do. Rather than me standing before them doing the teaching, I want to move the work from my hands into the arms of the kids. I am an adult—I want the kids to take it and run with their own ideas.

S: Is there an example of kids doing their own project and working with people who are different from them?

Jon: We have a bad conflict in Ukraine with the Russian War. We trained many kids who live in neighboring countries. One of those kids from a recent scout training in Poland was one of the first people at the border helping the refugees feel safe.

When UNICEF showed up they saw that the scouts were already there. These young scouts knew how to engage with others from different cultures and had already started setting up meeting points where people could come, rest and have a conversation if they were sad. They were helping the little children. Tough situations—but it is so impressive to see that kind of competence in the scouts.

Or someone who tells me that they are moving into politics to push positively to change something in the political system in Europe. My passion is to see people leave a training smiling and full of enthusiasm. Then I say, "Ok, we did something here—someone listened and understood how they could do something."

I was there, too, in my life. I was at a point when I met someone who introduced me to these tools. My life turned completely upside down in that moment when I said, "Yes that is where I can put myself into who I am!"

S: I think you just defined what a real teacher does. You ignite a positive spark in people, and you know when people feel an urgency to achieve their purpose. Igniting that spark is so important. Where does that spark come from and how can a teacher engage it? Is there a story about that?

Jon: I've been thinking how difficult it has been to be confined to online because I love being in the company of other people. I love being in a room with 20 people when I can focus on how people are feeling and can notice many things coming up. For example, I might see that someone is starting to sweat, and I ask them, what is it that is being said that is making you feel uncomfortable? It can really, really, really change something inside a person when I see them come out from feeling blocked, or pressured, or scared by someone saying something that is hurtful.

I had a situation last year about whether religion should be a big part of scouting. I had someone from a very Catholic group from Northern

Ireland and someone else from a very secular group in Belgium. That was conflicting. One person was harmful with their words because they didn't know how deeply the other person felt about their faith and that their words had harmed the other.

I had a young guy from Germany who was so insecure when he attended training in 2019. Today, he is one of the most promising young guys in World Scouting. He is standing on stages, giving strong positive vibes, and changing things as he goes along. He is grateful that we took him under our wing. After training, we also mentor people to help them take next steps. They can always reach out to us. We can talk to them about how they can move forward in the best way. It is so much work.

S: **It seems like your openness lets people go deeper. Is it your sincere curiosity that helps people learn more about themselves? How does that happen?**

Jon: Yes, how does that happen? I think you touched the right button about openness and a sense of confidentiality. There is a big level of trust. Trust is present without me saying it. I think my openness is clear to people. I'm always open to talk about anything.

S: **Sounds like you're not afraid to talk about emotions. Emotions are something you respect.**

Jon: Sure, I'm not scared of emotions … no, no, no. I could stand in front of a crowd talking about how to deal with trauma through arts. I could stand in front of a crowd and cry because it touched some deep feelings inside of me. No problem, that is life, it is just the way we are.

S: **When did you realize that underneath the good times growing up in your neighborhood there was also pain, conflict and hate speech? You saw suffering and meanness in many places. I'm curious how you dealt with that reality.**

Jon: Yes, and it can be very tough when you realize what is actually going on around you. Sometimes it can make me sick. Ok, we praise ourselves as open-minded—and yet we are still excluding some people, making all these differences among people, complaining about this and that, and badmouthing this and that.

Somehow this awareness made me surer about how I can change things by the way I am, by the way I talk with other people when others are watching. I made a conscious choice to be a positive example no matter the situation.

I want to show that a person can also be friendly, can be open and try to break down these negative vibes. I know there are systemic vibes that are impossible to break down because it comes from politicians. Regarding immigration, I can easily just say to people, don't look to Denmark! Look elsewhere if you want to know how to include refugees and migrants, because here it is not good. Find a better example.

S: I appreciate what you said about dealing with hatred and suffering by being a loving, connected, respectful presence wherever you are.

Jon: I have always been very stubborn. As a kid I was very shy, and I didn't want to look people in the eyes. I said at least if I have to meet a girl one day, I will need to look her in the eyes. I forced myself to look people in the eyes and now I cannot do anything else. If I want to change something positively, I go for it.

I have a lot of love. I have a love for my life. I have a lot of love for my fellow people on Earth here. While I love my country and where I live, I am not a nationalist! That is too closed!

S: What do you think ignites or nurtures that love you feel? Do you get off the path and do you need to reconnect with that deep love?

Jon: I don't feel like I get off the path. It's always on and … it's almost like art to me. I love the impressions, the colors of everything, the sounds and smells, the feelings of everything, the textures. I love to hug people because of the differences in people, and the smells … I paint and draw all kinds of everything and it's all very connected somehow. Just looking out the window I can see these beautiful green trees, the birds are singing, it is just, ahhhh … how magic is that?!

S: I think we are feeling it! The flowing love of the universe is just pouring through you. Do you know the writings of Rabindranath Tagore of India? He is ecstatic, elated, he is consumed with the vitality in life that is love and beauty. You remind me of his words. That's it, Jon! The flow of the interconnected power you have—it's love.

Jon: I love the idea of the democracy of the heart. It all starts there. The basic rhythm of everything, all music, all basic rhythm comes from the heart. We start there and we move, and we love and we share life, and what's not to love about it!

So much is about forgiveness. This flow that comes from forgiveness is one of the major things from my theological understanding. Jesus said it is all about forgiveness and love. God forgives. Why talk about hell when we can all be forgiven and enter heaven?

S: Yes, it is the lack of forgiveness that keeps us limited and wounded. I want to ask you about dialogue. You are a master facilitator of dialogue, especially in conflict situations. Is there a key learning to share about that?

Jon: A major thing I always emphasize is when to have dialogue and when absolutely not to dialogue. There will always be situations where conflict gets stuck. For example, take the war between Russia and Ukraine. Now there is no chance for dialogue at all. It will not help anything because there is full-on conflict and the only solution is that someone has to win, and someone has to lose. That is their only focus. There is no path for dialogue until both parties decide to dialogue. I always tell people that if you want to have dialogue with people in conflict it can only be fruitful if both sides agree to do so.

Otherwise, it will not be, it will be a win—lose situation. You will waste your time and your energy and maybe it will get worse.

I always start with people getting to know each other. The basics! If you don't know each other how can you have fruitful dialogue? I always have games where people have a chance to learn something about the other that they didn't know beforehand.

I will do something like that when I facilitate at a conference for religious leaders. I am considered something of a rascal. I like to stir things up a bit. Ok, you come to speak, and you come to say your things but how much do you know about the other people? How do you expect change to happen if you don't know who the other people are at this conference? The next time I'm going to introduce them to some of those games. It's impossible to dislike someone after you really establish a good relationship. It's all about relationships—human to human.

S: The work you do demands a high vision of what's possible. I want to ask you about "green shoots"—the good in people rising. Do you see "green shoots" and do you believe humanity can make it to a better place?

Jon: Absolutely! I'm very optimistic in that sense. Absolutely, we can make a difference. We should focus on the intergenerational approach. Even though the world is getting more open, and people communicate across countries, we are still very much, very much separated.

The older and the younger generations have completely different agendas. We can only move forward together. What keeps me in scouting is the vitality, the inspiration, the energy, the dynamics, and the will to change things and experiment with new ways; it's absolutely amazing! It keeps me young and keeps my mind thinking fresh! I hear something very interesting, and I say go with that!

Where are all the decision-makers? Let's mingle and do things together. Young people are gluing themselves to runways in airports because they want to make a statement that the politicians are not making. Why go to extremes? We could meet in the middle.

Every time I think I know something, someone younger than me shakes my world a bit and tells me that it is actually like this. It's about appreciating input from different people.

S: I'm excited to imagine thousands from younger and older generations coming up with ideas and solutions together. I want to ask you about a quote by an American writer, Terry Tempest Williams. She wrote, "the human heart is the first home of democracy." Do you have guidance about how we can build up the human heart?

Jon: It's kind of complicated, isn't it? It goes against the consumer-glamor industry that sells people on having everything and looking a certain way. All this effort only contributes to themselves.

I love my heart of course. I also need to give it away. It needs to get out of me. What use is it if it only stays inside of me? It is also meant to be shared with other people. Perhaps if we could wind back to when communities were smaller … but I won't talk about the old days, because things were not all good in the old days.

I like that quote. It reminds me of the triangle—educating mind, heart and hands. If we educate minds, hands and hearts we can have a more positive future. We can change things to be less from the mind and can become aware of how to change things from our heart—from love and compassion.

People have so much potential that is simply not unleashed. In life and in leadership if we look at them together, it is quite simple. If you narrow it down to the basics, it's very simple. Life happens. Leadership in life comes from the heart. People unnecessarily overcomplicate things. We should be able to listen to our heart. We don't need to complicate life with thinking that comes only from the mind; we need to come from the heart.

97

About Jon

Jon, a citizen of Denmark, is a seasoned dialogue peace trainer and facilitator. He has held leadership positions with the International World Scouts Movement, serving as a Diversity and Inclusion Consultant, as well as director of the Listening Ear project. He is currently the head of the World Scouts Dialogue for Peace Program that aims to make dialogue skills central in how scouts learn to live with diverse cultures and beliefs. Jon leads the Network for Dialogue, a program of an international interfaith organization, the King Abdullah bin Abdulaziz International Center for Interreligious and Intercultural Dialogue (KAICIID).

Jon dabbles in art for his own delight and holds dear his admiration of vintage cars. He sees himself always learning and relearning. Jon's humility and gratitude for life radiate love and hope in action in the positions he holds and with each person he meets along the way.

I love this idea of the democracy of the heart. It all starts there. The basic rhythm of everything, all music, all basic rhythm comes from the heart. We start there and we move, and we love, and we share life ... and what's not to love about it!

Thuy Duong Pham (Daisy)

Daisy takes the long view …

Supporting the birth of a new humanity actually happens with each person's individual transformation. That is what we can do.

Daisy and I participated in Peace Practice Alliance, a peacebuilding training program offered online by the Euphrates Institute of Peace. Her presence on the Zoom screen conveyed a bright spirit and quiet self-assurance. During our small group discussions, she spoke with joyful enthusiasm and simple authority. When considering people to include in this book, my intuition jumped to Daisy, but it was not because of the wisdom of her words or her work in Vietnam. I was curious about what made her face beam and the wellspring of her open spirit. I wanted to learn about how growing up in a country wounded by a treacherous ground war and dominated by an authoritarian government affected her adult choices and what gives meaning to her life.

Trying to find solutions for a world in crisis, in the early 2000s Daisy focused on sustainable development for her country. She found hope in the eco-village movement that offered a model for living in community that was harmonious with nature, peaceful, coherent and conscious.

Daisy takes the long view . . . she allows that it may take a thousand years for humanity to evolve toward the fulfillment of its spiritual destiny. Daisy is a steadfast explorer in the realms of esoteric philosophies, discovering along with fellow travelers that the best way to contribute to humanity's evolution is by changing one's own life.

S: Thank you, Daisy, for joining this exploration of new ways of being a human being. I think of this journey of discovery as the emerging, global heart of democracy—people all over the world who are choosing to act in service to the world from their deepest connection with spirit. I see you committed to this higher vision for humanity.

I only know your English name, Daisy. What is your Vietnamese name? Why did you choose the English name Daisy?

Daisy: In Vietnamese, my given name is Thuy Duong. It is the name of a kind of pine tree. My Vietnamese name starts with the sound "D," so I wanted to find an English name for a flower that starts with "D." For me, the daisy flower is a symbol of being free and wild and I wanted a name that was close to nature and was wild. I took the name Daisy when I was 22 and I started to study abroad.

S: When we met on a Zoom call, I was struck by your bright presence. You conveyed a feeling of inner knowing. Please tell me about what guided you to be who you are now?

Daisy: I'll start with my studies in university. I focused on environmental science and became interested in sustainable development. I wanted to contribute to the world to make it healthier, greener, happier. The deeper I went into this study I found that the ecological principles for sustainability are also the laws of nature.

Nature itself is the inspiration for sustainability. Tao is the way of nature, like what is written in the *Tao te Ching,* by Lao Tzu. When we follow the laws of nature, we thrive and survive. This sustains life in the long term. If we go against the laws of nature, we only destroy ourselves.

The more I think about this, I realize that the basic ecological principle is interconnectedness, called the web of life. It is a spiritual principle. It is about Oneness.

I'll read a quote from Vernon Howard, an American spiritual teacher and philosopher. His quote impressed me: "the great solution to all human problems is individual inner transformation."

It is about transformation of individual consciousness. It doesn't mean that we ignore national and environmental issues, the kind that Vietnam and other countries are facing such as: pollution, overconsumption, competition in economy, social problems and mental health issues.

Underneath all these problems that seem to be separate, we find that actually everything is interconnected.

The underlying issue is the problem of the individual's point of view. The point of view of each person evolves with time and with human progression. People's views will evolve from materialistic focus to spiritual focus. The more people expand their consciousness, the more they will be able to understand the views of others and the more they will come closer to the truth. Otherwise, the truth is hidden because the truth only comes forward from bringing together different points of view.

S: Your perception is that the challenges we are facing, like climate crisis, hunger, mental health and so on, are interrelated and arise out of human consciousness. Are you saying that people's consciousness must change for these problems to be resolved?

Daisy: Yes, when the consciousness of each person expands, they become personally transformed. This personal change will lead to the transformation of society and the world.

S: How did you come to understand this interconnected way of seeing? In your childhood did you have experiences close to nature that opened you to these insights?

Daisy: When I was ten years old, I read *Tao te Ching* by Lao Tzu and I sympathized with those ideas. It is about nature's way. Nature's way is the way of the universe. Lao Tzu taught three treasures that I continue to hold. They protect and enrich me:

Compassion – loving kindness

Simplicity – living simply, modestly and not wasteful

Humility – being truly humble. Humility can protect us. If we let the ego control us, it will lead us to grief, to an illusion of separateness and to the falsehood that we are the best. This is an illusion.

S: How did you learn about Tao Te Ching?

Daisy: Mostly from reading books. I read many commentaries and explanations of the Tao by great authors who explained it well. This learning touched me deeply.

S: I see you as a young girl, ten years old, drawn to this deep teaching. Were there signs that showed you that this was the path to follow?

Daisy: I'm not sure of other things but it was not only the Tao. Later I also studied Buddhism and then esoteric philosophy.

Beginning in 2015 I started to study esoteric philosophy, by another name it is called the Ageless Wisdom. It is not a religion but a synthesis of wisdom from many religions and teachings from the Masters. It is a combination of science, religion and philosophy. It provides a way of life and a way to evolve in our consciousness that purifies us and guides us to transform and serve the world. In our study we do not simply read books; we are encouraged to do three pillars as a disciple:

Study – contemplation of philosophy.

Meditation – the way that you connect to your higher self.

Service – to contribute, to help in any way, to practice what you have learned.

An aspirant is a truth seeker. A disciple is a more committed person on the path. As a disciple you commit to these three pillars, and you learn to listen to your own soul. Your first and your forever master is your own soul. Being a disciple does not mean that you follow an outside group or guru but becoming a disciple means that you are a student of your soul—you listen to your inner voice, your conscience.

S: **As you followed this path, did you run into doubts or barriers?**

Daisy: We are not alone on the path. We all have spirit guides. In the outer world we also have brothers and sisters on the path. In my city I have friends from the esoteric school. I consider them my brothers and sisters on the path.

I moved into this path naturally. My grandfather had a bookshelf. When I was in his house, I found these books and knew they were meant for older people, but I read them. I think the universe wanted me to have those books. They touched me ever since my childhood.

In my 20s, it was my ex-husband who introduced me to Buddhism. Learning with him was a second turning point for me. The way I approached Buddhism was not very religious but more about philosophy. I am not committed to a certain religion but rather as a free thinker. Growing up, I had no religion. I lived in a family that didn't really have religion, but we did worship our ancestors. I approached Buddhism in a more philosophical way, and I appreciate its wisdom. Buddhism explained many things to me.

In 2009, I got divorced and I was single for a long time. In 2014, I visited Plum Village, the community in France founded by Zen Master Thich Nhat Hanh. I loved the community there! It's like paradise, people are so kind and friendly. Nature is so beautiful, and I wanted to live happily like that and thought I would become a nun. Looking back, this was not a very mature decision because it was only the community life that attracted me to follow that life.

At this time, I know that I don't need to become a nun or live in a monastery. I can live a worldly life and still walk the path. I know that inner transformation is most important and that is my life's focus.

S: You mentioned that there is a Divine Plan that is leading to the birth of a new humanity, and it is in accord with the evolution of the human spirit. What is your vision for this birth of humanity?

Daisy: Let's talk about the vision for the birth of a new humanity. What I study in the teaching of the Masters and in other books is like this: The new humanity cooperates. They see human beings as one family. They see themselves as global citizens. They don't see separateness but honor the oneness of all.

They have the will to do good and act with a cooperative spirit. They have compassion and are sensitive to spirituality and sensitive to energy that they can send to others. They will have developed a sixth sense, their intuition. They will be able to sense one another and be very compassionate. They will have love for everyone and for nature. They love nature and they are joyful and are free spirits. They are not influenced by the masses but act from their own spirit and a deep sense of righteousness. They are honest and have a sense of inner and outer beauty and a feeling of harmony. That is the ideal.

S: I love this vision but so many people would say that it's not possible. On Earth, human beings cause problems and find misery and hardship. If this ideal seems so impossible, is it even worth having?

Daisy: Of course, the change cannot be overnight. It is a process of evolution. We are coming into the Aquarian Age and this age will cover the next more than 2000 years. But the birth of a new humanity has begun and is coming now. It is starting small, but it will grow and reach the final time in perhaps thousands of years. We are entering that age now.

S: Do you see signs of these things happening?

Daisy: Yes, for example, the group of participants from the global peace leadership course has participants from all over the world and they each really have love for humanity.

You know, the new human race will be different. We will refine this body and connect it with energy bodies within us. We won't be just the physical bodies we have now, but humans will also have access to higher, energetic bodies. Human beings will have refined "inner bodies" and will live with more virtues.

The evolution of consciousness is happening for everyone. Each person is developing at his or her own rate and is at different levels of consciousness. People will continue to purify and refine themselves.

S: **I'm curious if you see signs of this kind of change in Vietnam even in subtle ways. My sense is that it is out of sight.**

Daisy: At the moment we see more ugliness. We see things that make Earth depressed and that hurt us. Now we are the bottom of the materialistic way. The underlying motives are greed and corruption. Currently, things are quite ugly. It is not the vision, but we are in a transition toward the vision. Now the materialistic way is in the forefront. The Earth is at the very bottom now—when we see many bad things. We see war, separateness, hatred, dangerous climate change and environmental pollution. But because we are at the bottom, it will go up and things will change for the better.

I still believe in the good. It is like the laws of karma. We are still receiving the fruits of all the bad things and these bad fruits of past wrongs are displaying. People are suffering and people will learn from old mistakes. Even though it is painful, these bad things must happen, and people can learn from the pain and suffering.

Also in this time, we can see signs that give hope. During Covid time, we saw many people with good will and people whose hearts were kindled with compassion. People are going inward to reflect on what is important to life—what really matters. They are becoming more spiritual. So, among the chaos and ugliness and the bad things, we still see hope in the people with the will to do good.

S: **It takes strength to see through the darkness and believe that there is an opening for the good to break through. What helps you and others continue to have active hope in the face of so many ugly things?**

Daisy: We read the teaching. The teaching tells us that it is important to keep the five Ds:

Discipline – for the physical body to eat well, sleep well, exercise.

Dispassionate – for the emotional body to stay calm and free from personal bias.

Discrimination – for the mental body to choose between what is good and what is bad.

De-centralization – for the personality to shift focus of attention from "me" to focus on others.

Detachment – is for the soul so that we live in the world fully and let go of outcomes. We try our best and detach from the result; detach from the external world and live more from the inner world, the world of meaning, eternal values, the world of causes.

Disciples need to look deeper into the root causes of what is happening and we must look further ahead to see how things happening now will impact the future. We need to keep having cool heads and warm hearts.

When I saw they had cut the forest, I was so angry. I tried to overcome it through patience. That is the way we bring balance to the Earth. When we meditate, we come to our root core, our inner being, and that is the source of love, healing, joy. The source of all that connects us with all that is.

I can feel detached from the phenomenal world. The Earth is a school for the soul. Whatever happens here is for us to learn. We detach from the phenomenal and we see the root causes, we see the effects of what happens now far into the future. We see beyond the chaos, and we keep detached and trust in the Divine. Everything happens for a reason, so it is important that we learn from each situation and not get emotionally attached. Then, we can move on.

S: **For people who feel pushed and pulled this way and that, how do you encourage them to stay on the path?**

Daisy: I understand because walking the path is not an easy job. There are many challenges, but the reward is worth it. Not everyone needs to be on the path at the same time. We need to respect each person's own story, each person's own evolution. People need to experience life in their own way, as young souls, not in biological age, but in the age of their soul. When a young soul comes to the Earth, they must experience life, first. To walk on the path and awaken is for old souls who have accumulated wisdom from all the mistakes and experiences in their past lives.

We can't push someone to choose the path when they have not had much experience. We learn from mistakes and failures more than successes. Of course, we appreciate our successes, but the point is that mistakes and failures give us precious lessons to learn.

If we push someone too soon, it is not good for them. It forces them and it is not natural. They need to draw wisdom from their own experience which is the more natural way. We don't force anyone. If it comes it comes at the right time for the right person.

S: You are speaking as a wise teacher. What is your plan for yourself? Do you see yourself growing as a spiritual teacher?

Daisy: Education and healing are the work that I am most interested in. Healing isn't about being a doctor in a hospital but healing means making whole. The healer is the one who helps others integrate everything. Healing is more about spiritual life.

Now, old souls are coming to an end of their evolution as members of the human kingdom. They are coming into the spiritual kingdom or the soul kingdom. That means we bring heaven on Earth. That means that human beings in the future will enter into Earth as the kingdom of the soul. Our job is to actualize this soul kingdom on Earth.

S: Thich Nhat Hanh said, "paradise est ici." Paradise is here. Heaven is already here on Earth; heaven is among us.

Daisy: Yes, it is a matter of consciousness, the Christ consciousness. It is an inclusive, soul consciousness that is joyful and loving. With this soul consciousness we live in paradise. If we keep low, negative feelings, greed, hatred and illusion, then that is hell.

S: Each person has the freedom to make choices every single minute that determines where they are, heaven or hell.

Daisy: People make choices to go forward into the light.

S: When you work with people, what is it you do? Is it one on one or group work?

Daisy: It is group work. Group work is the methodology of the new age. In the old age we worked separately, but the Aquarian age is the age of fellowship and we understand that a group has higher efficiency.

For example, if we have ten people in our group it is not just ten units of energy and power. The power of a united group of ten people is bigger than the sum of ten individuals. A group creates its own entity that has its own soul. There is harmony within a group soul. It is like that.

When we meditate together, we feel that group-soul feeling. We feel support from our brothers and sisters in the group. It's better when we are physically together but sometimes, we are just online.

I really appreciate your work with Global Meditation Gathering each week. It's wonderful that people are coming together with goodwill and kind hearts. That group energy is powerful.

S: As you describe group-soul energy, it supports the idea in democracy that all voices are valued. Every person's energy counts. When a group centers with spirit, issues can be resolved better. Groups that find unexpected harmony when they act together is one way I see the heart of democracy arising. What do you think about this idea that there is a heart of democracy arising in the world?

Daisy: I very much believe in this vision because it is so aligned with the teaching that humanity is one. The soul of humanity is in the process of birthing. Now, humanity is being seen simply as a "personality"—this is a manifestation of the lower self; but the soul, or the higher self of humanity, is coming. It is in process. It is coming through people who live with compassion and the will to do good. We need to nurture this process in people. We need to support the birthing of the soul of humanity.

S: What is your advice for how people can support this process of birthing the soul of humanity?

Daisy: To help the birthing of the soul of humanity, first, we must find each other and come together. Like-minded people and people of good will need to come together everywhere. Form groups, meditate together, work and talk together to enhance the connections with each other. Sally, what you are doing is exactly aligned with the divine plan.

S: Thank you for saying that.

Daisy: To meditate with a group is best but to meditate individually, every day is also good. Living meditation is to be mindful in our daily life. It is not necessary to sit alone, we can be mindful anywhere at any time. Keeping mindfulness in your life is a way that we come closer to the real "thinker" in us, our soul. Through meditation we align ourselves with our soul. At the soul level, there is oneness; it is not your soul or my soul, but we are one soul.

Of course, in one way, we each have our unique soul, but in another way, we are not separate souls. At this level there is only one soul. So, we meditate to connect with our own soul and then we are already nurturing our connection with the one soul of humanity. Supporting the birth of a new humanity happens with each person's individual transformation. That is what we can do.

We connect with like-minded people, meditate in a group, do good things, and study the wisdom.

Most important is meditation. Through meditation you can connect to your higher self. True meditation has many effects—it purifies your mental and emotional body; it makes you calmer and wiser. Also, it helps you to develop intuition. Intuition is a high-level function. It is not a gut feeling from the lower chakra, but it is a very high level of consciousness.

S: **It is through meditation that we deeply connect to the fullness of who we are. Transformation doesn't happen in busyness, or achievements, but from the stillness of going inside oneself.**

Daisy: Yes, transformation comes through study and contemplation of wise teaching, meditation and service. Through serving we learn many things: we integrate what we study and what we receive in meditation. We also accumulate the merits of service. Those merits will help open our minds. Everything is interrelated. Serving is the work of love and we need to display it. When you display your love through service you manifest your soul.

S: **You are sharing precious wisdom about things happening in our midst. But people are also struggling to find a helpful path and walk it. What words of encouragement can you offer to ordinary people who want to step on a spiritual path but don't know how?**

Daisy: I think that if I can say anything to encourage people, it may be to try and listen to your inner voice. Listen to the voice of silence. You really have to feel it because this voice speaks softly. Listen to your voice, not to the lower self, but to your true self. Listen to it and live with it.

When you do something that gives you real joy, you satisfy your soul. Joy is the quality of the soul.

It is so easy for the lower self to command our attention, but you must listen to the softer, inner voice in silence and do what makes you feel joyful and happy from your heart. That is what your soul wants.

Live as a soul and treat others as a soul. Of course, people have a lower self, and they can act ugly; but we can choose to see their potential and respect this potential and not get stuck judging their current state. Nurture the good qualities in others and in yourself. See people as souls and live as a soul. It is easy to forget to live as a soul every day, but as much as possible, we can try to live as a soul and treat others as a soul.

S: What you say is very true for me. Thank you for reminding me that it takes sincere daily commitment and dedication.

About Daisy

Daisy was born in Ho Chi Minh City (formerly Saigon) in 1979 during a time when Vietnam was united under the communist regime of the North and when government subsidies barely kept millions of people alive. Her life in Vietnam became more economically secure during her growing up years.

As a life-long learner, community server, truth seeker and spiritual practitioner, she is passionate about ageless wisdom, esoteric philosophy and the universal laws of life. She is also interested in holistic education, green living and sustainable development.

Daisy received her BA degree in Environmental Engineering from Ho Chi Minh City University of Technology, a MS in Environmental and Resource Management from Brandenburg Technical University in Germany, a MSc in Urban Development from Vietnamese-German University, and a PhD from Lappeenranta University of Technology in Finland.

She has worked as a technical officer for GIZ in an environment project in the Mekong Delta and joined a fellowship at Teach for Vietnam. Currently, she is working as translator and mentor for the Vietnamese program at the Morya Federation Esoteric School. She is also studying and doing research in esoteric philosophy and has her YouTube channel *Soul Space*.

I think that if I can say anything to encourage people, it may be to try and listen to your inner voice. Listen to the voice of silence.

Audrey Lin

There really is a quiet revolution happening in so many corners of the world from everyday people who live in different ways, who have different faith backgrounds and traditions, who work in different fields. These are people who believe in love, in compassion, in stillness, in service.

There is an incredible power that can flow through us when we are not focused on ourselves.

Audrey speaks with modest laughter and smiling eyes. We first met in person at a restaurant in Berkeley, California, when she invited me to attend Karma Kitchen. Inspired by ServiceSpace, Karma Kitchen is a worldwide movement spreading smiles, sharing insights and generating a culture of generosity. Volunteers take over a restaurant for a day and run it with different rules. Guests are given a Smile Card that says, "SMILE, you've been tagged, pay it forward." You don't pay for your meal because someone before has paid for you.

Later, Audrey taught me about "laddership" as a way of leading. I quickly recognized that she embodies the qualities of "laddership" that she nurtures in others. Laddership is about courage, fulfillment and joy through invisible service; bowing down to something greater than yourself, creating context for transformation, holding emptiness for what is emerging.

Reflecting on deeper democracy, Audrey said, "It's about a different understanding of power. There is an incredible power that can flow through us when we are not focused on ourselves. Like when we are thinking of a greater whole when we are thinking of somebody else."

S: Thank you, Audrey, for speaking with me about a subject close to my heart that I call the global heart of democracy. I see the potential for human beings to live from a deeper dimension that is in right relationship with each other and the planet. This potential arises from an indomitable human spirit inside us.

I'm hoping that lifting up stories of people who are living this truth can guide the rest of us along this path. I see you as one of those people. I see a smiling presence, a confident joy, a sense of inner knowing. How do you see yourself and how would you say you arrived at this way of being?

Audrey: I'm just a very confused person going along on this mysterious life path. Maybe it started as a teenager, holding questions like, "What is the point of everything? What's the meaning of it?"

I was blessed with parents who really cared about me, worked hard to provide whatever they could for their children. In that context, there is such a focus on getting everything materially, especially in the U.S. where there is such an emphasis on material security and success. I just remember as a young person feeling very empty, and feeling there must be more. It's great to have things, and we weren't wealthy. I lived the suburban lifestyle where everything is in strip malls, and you have a house and a yard—I felt like there has to be a deeper purpose.

I grew up with no religion. My parents were scientists. They were immigrants from Taiwan. They weren't even Buddhists. I grew up in an agnostic environment on the East Coast, surrounded by a lot of friends. There was a lot of Christianity. My best friend was Jewish. I remember going to the temple with her. Pretty awesome, actually.

I remember in college being really curious about different faith traditions. I wanted to learn more about why we are what we are and what drives us. I looked into religion and physics and philosophy. Ultimately, I landed at service and stillness. It wasn't a particular institution, not a particular theory of the world. It was more about the small practices of being of service to other living beings in the world and finding space to tap into an inner sense of myself.

S: Those are beautiful words together, "service and stillness." Was it by lived experience that you arrived at that synthesis of these words, "let me be still and let me be of service?"

Audrey: When I was in college I was drawn to learn about different social issues. I felt it in my heart—"I really want to help! I want to help figure out educational inequality! I want to help figure out poverty!"
All these big things you throw around when you are in college—these big, lofty world things. I remember thinking, "I really want to do something about all of this!"

And so, I tried. I got involved with different groups. I got involved in different efforts. And then after some time, I felt like everybody was fighting for peace. Everybody was blaming some group, some system. There wasn't a sense of how we can collectively rise up. It was a critical, academic environment—that's natural, right? It fosters critical thinking.

Then I thought, "I have to learn about Gandhi. I must learn about Martin Luther King Jr. I have to learn about different non-violent leaders who really embody the change they wish to see. That year, I happened to find this small organization that was hosting a non-violence mentorship program. Ten young people in their twenties were participating in this program where they would intern four days a week with a local non-profit organization. On Fridays we would all come together and have workshops on non-violence and learn different things. In that program I learned a lot about Gandhi, and I learned about meditation. That was where the meditation piece came in.

And then the service... I had always learned about service as "haves" helping the "have-nots—and seeing it as an action-based thing in the world. That summer I stumbled across this small meditation circle in the family home of Nipun Mehta, whom you know. Now these kinds of gatherings are called Awakin Circles (awakening with kin).

At that time, they were just called Wednesdays. People would come, sit in silence for an hour, and there would be a wisdom reading of a few paragraphs from different wisdom traditions. Then we'd go around the circle and share different reflections that came to mind. In the last hour, this amazing woman, Harshida, would offer dinner for everybody. When they started, there were only three people. By the time I was going there were 20 or 30 people going every week. Before the pandemic they had to cap it at 66 people. That's when the wait list started.
It was a simple, simple space. It was so simple, you could miss the beauty, the extraordinariness of it. It was just people sitting in silence for an hour; people listening to each other for an hour, sharing their reflections on their

life journeys, and this offering of a home-cooked dinner for everybody. I remember thinking the first time—I was a twenty-year-old in college—how does this help homeless people? That's where my mind was at the time. How can we solve inequalities like this?

S: How did you answer your own question?

Audrey: I didn't have an answer. I thought, "Okay, this doesn't help homeless people, but for some reason I feel good when I come, and I'm learning when I come." So, I kept going.

Over time, I started to feel like these people know something I don't know. There was an inner groundedness in people that I would meet in these spaces. It wasn't shiny. I was used to a world where everything is marketed to me, and I was marketing things to other people, "Have you tried this? Well, you need this!" . . . a gimmicky type of narrative. In this space, I was entering a family home, there was the simplicity of that.

At the end of that summer, a few people from that group were reopening Karma Kitchen, which is a "pay it forward" restaurant—one of the projects of ServiceSpace. They had started it a year or two before, then the restaurant owner changed, and so they were reopening it. I volunteered for the reopening day. It was a Sunday. Our focus was trying to make people smile.

S: It wasn't long after that I stumbled in there and met you. I felt the spirit!

Audrey: Right! Doesn't it take 10,000 hours to master something? Imagine if you spent 10,000 hours trying to make people smile. We never think to do that. A doctor will spend thousands of hours practicing surgery. An athlete will spend tens of thousands of hours doing drills and perfecting themselves physically. What if we exercise that muscle to tune into what other people would want and what they're feeling and how we can support them and lift them up because we see their shared humanity? My lifting up is bound to your lifting up.

S: I realize you weren't asking just as individuals with that intention to make people smile, but you had a group ethos. You knew that was a shared focus of intention.

Audrey: Right! You're not the only crazy person to make someone smile. And there was the shared stillness. That's a very powerful feeling for me, to sit with other people in stillness, where everyone is looking within for an hour. And we practiced in a group every week at Karma Kitchen. We were 10 to 15 volunteers, everyone wanting to grow in service, to make people smile. We were tapping into this regenerative force within ourselves.

You're not expecting an end result. You're really looking at cultivating the quality of compassion, the quality of service and stillness and that spirit within it. The outcomes are a byproduct of the depth with which you cultivate that quality. Outcomes will naturally follow. Instead of focusing on serving 'x' number of pay it forward meals—because you can get focused on that metric—if you fine tune that quality and cultivate those service muscles within yourself, the end result of serving growing numbers of people will naturally happen.

S: You said several revolutionary ideas that could turn current patterns of valuing and behaving upside down. You said that "simplicity can mask the extraordinary." What a wonderful piece of wisdom that is. There is extraordinary in the simple. We're not trained to see that.

Whether you are practicing stillness or acts of service, it's the purity of that gesture and that clarity of intention that emerges among people who know that's what they're doing. What a powerful way to get results—when you're not thinking about results.

Audrey: And it's a group of imperfect people. It's not like you're trying to be a saint, you're just trying to practice in a group.

S: Let's go a bit further into the quality of stillness. Many people say, "I'm too busy to be still. I have important things to do. I get too fidgety." Say a little more about how you help people to bridge into stillness.

Audrey: I feel like stillness has really become a teacher for me. But I've spoken with a friend who says, "That's not my path." Our minds are wired in different ways. But I do feel that for many people stillness can be a great teacher. Different forms of stillness, even if it's just five minutes—it doesn't have to be an hour. Before I even knew what stillness was, before I was even introduced to meditation, my stillness was going for a run in nature. That would quiet my mind.

Meditation taught me the practice of observing and accepting whatever arises. I practiced refining that awareness to be able to see things without as much reactivity and without as many filters. I think stillness is a great tool to help us see more clearly. It is to help us clean our lenses—like spring cleaning for the mind. At the same time, I think there are many paths for many different minds. Everyone has to find what works for them.

I do feel it's a beautiful thing to be introduced to stillness. Even if it's not every person's path, just to have the exposure is a powerful thing. I remember years ago working at a school where we practiced mindfulness with the students during detention time. It was so beautiful to see how some of those kids responded to it. It's powerful to see the natural quality of stillness recognized in a person when they are given the space to be still. Today we are constantly being bombarded with so many messages, so many things that we have to be, so many devices, so many things in our minds vying for our attention. To be invited to be still, to observe, even for two minutes, that's definitely something we could use more of.

S: **What you say about stillness resonates with me. It doesn't need to take a long time. Even a moment of stillness has so much potential to create a shift.**

Audrey: I was introduced to stillness for the first time when I was a college student. We were in a small seminar class and the professor would start each class with a few minutes of what he called 'arriving'—which is basically silence. The way he framed it was that it takes time for our minds to catch up with our bodies. Even though our bodies are in this room, our minds might be in many different places. So, we need to take a few minutes to let our minds fully arrive and become ready to do the work we have to do in this space. I remember viscerally the difference between times when I would come into that class late, with my mind in so many directions, versus when I would sit down in that class and have a few minutes to 'arrive.' I remember how clear my mind would be for the 90 minutes of that class. How much more focused I was because I had that space, those few minutes, to fully arrive.

S: **I love how little fixes can make big shifts in us. Let's talk about another shift. You said we have enough leaders in our world but not enough 'ladders'. You started a whole movement, called "laddership." Please tell me about "laddership" and what you are learning.**

Audrey: In a funny way, it's something that's as old as the hills, and I was definitely just one part of many people's experience, many "ladders."

First, the laddership term came up eleven years ago with this amazing man, Jayesh Patel. He grew up in the Gandhi ashram at Gujarat in India. He is a true servant leader, a true ladder in many ways, nurturing so many people.

He was visiting the U.S. and ServiceSpace volunteers were having a team leader retreat, where they were sharing what they had been learning and what had unfolded throughout the year. They asked him if he wanted to come, and he said, "Leader—I don't want to be a leader. I want to be a "ladder." He is the king of puns, so he was always saying things like that. Everyone said, "that's what we want, too. We want to be ladders. It's a team laddership retreat!" So, that's where the concept of laddership first came up.

Some years later, programs to nurture a field of generosity entrepreneurs began to surface. ServiceSpace has been volunteer-run for many years and has been incubating many labors of love efforts. Along the way there are so many people asking … whether it's in education, business, filmmaking, art, politics—how can I lead with love? How can I really embody my values through my work and not end up sacrificing some part of myself?

Inner transformation is not something you can copy. It's unique to each person's nature. You can't really have an equation for it. There's no recipe. No five steps you take to lead from inner transformation. It's unique to who you are, unique to your context, your project, your intentions, your community—everything. We recognized that a lot of people were asking this question, so we thought that maybe what we can do is come together in a circle and hold these questions together and experiment together and share with each other. That's how we started the Laddership Circles in 2015.

They were just small circles, ranging from six to twenty people. We had a six-week curriculum where we would look at different themes and have different practices—head, hand, heart curriculum. We engaged in practices for the hands. We read and watched different content pieces for the head. Then with your heart you would reflect and share with others. It was a learning program to explore different organizing principles around leading with inner transformation, leading with love, and designing for generosity. So different experiments rippled out on their own and it was beautiful.

When the pandemic hit, suddenly so many people were asking these questions and so many people had screen time, so we built a "laddership pod" to make it available to more people.

Laddership doesn't require doing a project. It's a way of seeing and a way of being, and there's different ways of doing that.

S: These are key ideas . . . leading with love, finding one's personal ways of doing that, realizing that everyone's contribution is part of the big picture. I'm learning from you that each person needs to find his/her own way of personal transformation and learning how to work in a group.

I'm curious about your experience of the scale of ServiceSpace. Hundreds of people sign up to participate in these programs. These big numbers of people showing up could be an amazing sign of what is possible for humanity. Please say more about what this huge scale is teaching you.

Audrey: Scale happens in nature, like how the seeds of a dandelion flower will travel and will surface. It's more like when you see weeds in your garden that have suddenly scaled. The process of giving service is less a factory model and more of a gardening model. When you are sowing seeds and when you keep sowing seeds, and the conditions are right, and you work hard to sow them, they will take off in a way that a factory could not produce using a linear approach to increasing scale.

ServiceSpace doesn't really do outreach things. Often it is more of a pull than a push. We don't do recruiting. Instead of pushing forward this project or vision to those who would want to participate, it is more of a pull. In ServiceSpace we say things like, "Oh, somebody expressed interest in this topic and creating a gathering space, we can build a circle around this idea and see what comes up in our collective consciousness." From there, people are naturally pulled in that direction and then so many other things surface.

So, it is moving from a "plan and execute" model to a "search and amplify" process. Typically, you plan and execute a plan or a project. That is normal and planning is a core part. You need to have some planning and have some way of executing something.

But one thing I have learned in the "search and amplify" process is that you are not just projecting this vision into a vacuum or to these unknown audiences, but what you are really doing is building context with a lot of different people in different ways based on what is moving within them.

You are also saying that "I assume there is value in every person and every living thing in every situation; and you are asking how can I have eyes to see that value and amplify those patterns and positive potentials?" It's really a process of building context with a person or a group and coming from that shared context where everyone is wanting to contribute.

You can come in wanting to learn something or to get something, but it is not just a transactional thing. You are coming together as a volunteer and entering a way of co-creation. Instead of focusing only on content, and especially online programs do focus on content, it is about creating a container to hold that content and actually live it out.

I remember one of many instances that touched me was when we had a "Living and Dying Pod." It was a weeklong online learning, and each day's learning was powerful. Each day had different themes. Some were: "Graceful Exits" and the "Sacred Work of Grief." This happened during the pandemic, so it was relevant for people.

At the end of it there was a guest speaker and she had done a lot of work with prayer. She had all of us create prayer mandalas. At the end, one person in the group created a mandala using sidewalk chalk. She lived on a cul-de-sac and decided to create a mandala on the street. She shared the photo of the mandala, and it was a beautiful thing. Another participant in the Pod saw that chalk mandala and she was deeply moved. She had just learned that a friend of hers had passed away. After seeing that chalk mandala, she decided to make her own and dedicate it to her friend who had passed away and to her friend's family. This was such a beautiful example of how what one person does ripples into what someone else does. And those are just the ripples we see! It is a beautiful flow.

S: That sounds like the dandelion you spoke about. A seed goes out into the world and naturally, without intentional effort, more seeds blossom. You don't know exactly where the seeds will land or how they will give life in a new place.

Audrey: Yes, you can't predict it but you are ready for it, you tune into it and you put your wind behind it when you can, and it grows into whatever force it wants to take on its own.

S: There is so much wisdom in what ServiceSpace does that can change how people operate in the world. Are there specific ideas in what ServiceSpace does that you cherish, that you are passionate about?

Audrey: One thing that comes to mind at this moment is the emptiness of it. Not emptiness in a cold, lonely way, but emptiness as formlessness. All these projects have surfaced in such beautiful ways. A lot of our initial ideas were just to make people smile, but from there an initial idea naturally turned into a project.

What I really appreciate is the formlessness. ServiceSpace is really just a rotating group of volunteers who put their offering into it. Some projects come and some go. There isn't a need for it to be institutionalized or to be set in a certain way. There is no sense of permanence because it is so living! It's so alive! Love is alive. Compassion is alive. You can't make it into a static thing, you can't make it a static product. It is a spirit.

I really appreciate how every Awakin Circle, every event, every Pod, everything is just a snapshot of a unique configuration in the moment that it came together to express stillness and service in that way. It happens in that way, and then that energy goes out to find a different form.

For example, even now Nipun and all these volunteers have started a ServiceSpace GPT and are focusing on how all this artificial intelligence stuff can be used for service. That surfaced in the context of these times. So, it is not about sticking to a certain form, but it's about being fluid and developing with the times and finding unique manifestations of service in different contexts.

S: How do you see this way making impact in the world? Do you think it can change the patterns of ownership and linear project development? How can these revolutionary ideas and experiments penetrate the status quo?

Audrey: Service is a quality. It is not a company or project, but it is a characteristic of life force that is translatable everywhere. Even in ServiceSpace, people honestly just need some name or some format for the mind to conceptualize what it is, but "service" is really so many things.

I think that the impact is a quiet, invisible thing around the world. There really is a quiet revolution happening in so many corners of the world from everyday people who live in different ways, who have different faith backgrounds and traditions, who work in different fields. These are people who believe in love, in compassion, in stillness, in service. They are bringing these basic human qualities out in their own ways.

One of our ServiceSpace volunteers runs a huge business; long ago, employees in his business were like 2500. He was the CEO. He is literally the person who at ServiceSpace retreats is the chauffeur who picks people up at the airport. He is the menu planner. He is a hot-shot CEO, and he acts from these service-oriented values. These ancient values are powerful! As Gandhi said, "Truth and non-violence are as old as the hills." I have immense faith in the scale of those words.

Most people are trained to think of scale in linear ways. But we don't know what we don't know. There is so much going on that I can't begin to fully comprehend the way the world works and the ways that the mysteries of our cosmos are organized.

We can't even begin to know all of that. Knowing that I have my blind spots, I do have joy in these practices of kindness, in these practices of service. I feel that for me, these are small little windows, little entries into the mysteries of the universe.

S: Let's look at what these ideas have to do with the spirit of democracy. I sense there is this urge, a divine plan for human beings to serve the world and fulfill their hearts. When you think about connecting personal transformation with democracy, what comes to your mind?

Audrey: Wow—democracy. I'm no expert. But I just googled it (laughs) and the definition I found is: "Democracy is a system of government where state power is vested in the people, or the general population of a state, based on principles of liberty and free will."

I think we have to change the way we look at power. In one of our Laddership Pods we have a curriculum module where we talk about power. And we read this article about different forms of power: power over, power with, and power within.

I think there is an incredible power that can flow through us when we are not focused on ourselves. Like when we are thinking of a greater whole and when we are thinking of somebody else. There is a deeper form of power that we become a part of. It's like a murmuration of starlings, right?

Not about any singular person, or any singular being even; it is just in the space between each of us. There is a greater wisdom with a beat that we are marching to.

There is research on how a murmuration of starlings work. Each starling just keeps track of the seven starlings closest to it. If every starling keeps track of the seven starlings closest to it, they form these beautiful swarms, these eloquent ways of flying together. So, it's not necessarily about focusing on numbers, masses of people. In fact, you can break a lot by doing things that way because you are just looking at statistics and you are not looking at the stories behind the statistics.

But if each person focuses on the seven people closest to them and trusts in the power of compassion, in the power of virtues, in the power of these shared human values to hold and support each other, that is a deeper kind of power vested in the people. This is when we can really be of support to each other, and we can grow in different ways. It's hard for me to be theoretical about it. So much is grounded in what we experience in regular life.

S: To focus a minute on "regular life," what would you say to the 7th and 8th graders you are teaching now about what gives you meaning? What are practical things you live by that you would like to share with others?

Audrey: I was struck a few months ago when the U.S. Surgeon General said that we are living in an epidemic of loneliness. Part of the reason I am drawn to youth now is because of the mental health concerns I have heard about the pandemic's effect on youth.

During the pandemic, I would feel the fullest when I had someone to give to, when I had dishes to do for someone, someone to make tea for, somebody to show up for. We can't underestimate the power of just showing up for other people in whatever form it is. It really is part of the thread that keeps us all alive and connected.

On a practical level, I just do acts of kindness. When I am having a bad day, I tell myself that I need to do a random act of kindness because I'm getting too much into my own problems. When I'm strong enough I force myself to go out and do random acts of kindness and it totally shifts everything. Without fail, it completely changes how I see myself, how I see others, how I see the world, how I see life.

S: So simple, in all the complexity. You are teaching me that when we recognize the source of our true power, we can create a deeper meaning of democracy, a new way to use our personal freedom.

Would you like to say anything more before we close?

Audrey: I feel grateful, and thank you, Sally, for holding space for this conversation and for exploring these notions of democracy in a different way. That gives me inspiration and hope. I'm glad to know you are there, a person of good heart, shining where you are, and nurturing this offering for the world.

S: I love the way murmurations work. It's enough to connect with a small cluster of people, like the fourteen people gathered in this book. Unexpected outcomes may come from lifting up just a few people who have clarity about the meaning of their own lives and who are connected to something more. Thank you, Audrey.

About Audrey

Not content just to read about the spiritual practices of peace leaders like Gandhi and Martin Luther King Jr., Audrey decided to take a walking pilgrimage of 50 miles from the University of California in Berkeley to a friend's home in Santa Clara, CA. Audrey is admired for walking her talk. It is not enough for her to have good values or admire values in others, but she is determined to live her values with simplicity, courage and practical wisdom.

Audrey's earliest dream was to be an artist and she even considered being a hermit. In college at the University of California, Berkeley, she participated in the Metta Center for Non-Violence Education. After meeting Nipun Mehta and attending Awakin Circles in his parent's home, she spent several years developing transformational programs with the ServiceSpace community. Audrey's "laddership" in service to others was so generous, graceful and wise that she gained a huge global fan club! Audrey's article, "Deep Dive into the Gift Ecology" and her Ted Talk, "Experiments in Kindness," as well as other insights are available in her online interviews and podcasts.

Currently, Audrey is teaching middle grade students in San Francisco. She is grounded in the truth that in the end there is only kindness.

During the pandemic, I would feel the fullest was when I had someone to give to, when I had dishes to do for someone, someone to make tea for, somebody to show up for. We can't underestimate the power of just showing up for other people in whatever form it is. It really is part of the thread that keeps us all alive and connected.

Biswadeb Chakraborty

We are meant to live so that others may live;
part of the elegant harmony of life.

I met Biswadeb in California in 1997 at a meeting to launch a new global interfaith organization, United Religions Initiative (URI). All of us who gathered at Stanford University for the planning meetings were passionate about the opportunity to create something that had never happened before. We envisioned people of diverse religions, spiritual expressions and indigenous traditions all over the world cooperating for the common good. Biswadeb, 25 years old at the time, captivated the assembly with his soaring tabla drumming. We surprised ourselves with the joy of unexpected friendships with people from different backgrounds. Imams and nuns, bankers and philosophers, organization consultants, teachers and teenage activists came together united in this "far out" vision. With infectious warmth and willingness to do whatever it took, Biswadeb committed his life to building bridges among people so that "the other" becomes "a brother."

During the ensuing 25+ years with URI, we worked with people around the world developing URI as a locally rooted and globally connected multi-cultural organization. Biswadeb could have veered to a more lucrative, less controversial and prestigious career path, but he did not. As the URI community grew to over a thousand local grassroots activist groups, Biswadeb deepened the URI community's understanding of the concept "Ektaan"—One Tone. His life bears witness to the truth that underlying differences, a cosmic rhythm beats in the hearts of humanity. We are meant to live so that others may live; part of the elegant harmony of life.

S: I have observed your commitment to a life of service. You care about building up others and pushing for what is fair and just. What were the turning points in your life that guided you to this commitment to service?

Biswadeb: Sally, our years working together seem like a blink of an eye but every moment I have had working with you is vivid. It is the experience of unconditional love and affection that we hold for the whole universe and for each other. I am still on a quest to know about myself and discover answers to the big question, "Who am I?" So, I feel it is so relevant that I speak with you in this moment,

I see that being born into my family was spiritual karma. I was born in a rural village in West Bengal, India. My father worked as a chemist and had the financial ability to put me in a good school. Our village had priority to give education to the boys, not the girls. My sisters had some schooling but got married before they finished their education. As a child I wanted to spend more time with my mother but could not.

I was six when my father brought me out of the village to live with him and go to school. I lived with my father and a cook and caretaker, and I missed my mother so terribly. I still remember those moments. On weekends I would go home but early Monday mornings I had to go back to school, and I didn't like that at all.

Living with my father allowed me to embrace the people who came to see him. He was also a guru, a practicing yogi. People came to see him but couldn't offer food to my father so they would give food to me. They cared for me and took me on their laps. There were so many people who came into my life at that time.

My life was so different than if I had just stayed at home with my mother and sisters. Nearly 100 people would come to see my father for prayers on Saturday evenings. I missed my mother, but I had all the love and affection from all those people in my life. As a child it was my life to be open to people and have a lot of affection for people.

When I was fourteen, I developed a relationship with many of my father's disciples. I went to their homes on weekends. My mother took care of my ancestral home in the village; both mother and father sacrificed so much. Now I am thankful that I went to a good school, but I could not see the benefit at the time. I could only see me missing my mother. I thought my father did not do the right thing.

S: What was it about your mom that you wanted so much to be with her?

Biswadeb: I was born during the communist movement in my country and there was much unrest. It was difficult because we were a Brahman family, and Brahmans were treated badly by the communists. They took land and made life hard. There were arrests and violence. The moment the communists started ruling in the state in 1971-72, my mom chose to stay and protect the land. My father could not go to that village because he had his spiritual responsibilities. My mother had to stay and fight to keep the land. She fought so strongly, she fought with everyone—the police, the communists. I loved that part of mother. My mother would take me on her lap and feed me and cuddle me and I missed that.

We were isolated, we were the only Brahmans who lived in that area of the village where lower caste people lived. Now I see it as a gift, but other Brahmans would not come to our home because we lived in a place nearby lower-caste people.

I always wanted to play with the children who were lower-caste and people would say no. Many times, I would go secretly to a field and lake, and I played with those children. Then others would complain to my mother that she should bathe me because I had been playing with "untouchable" children. My mother would tell me it's ok. She would shout at me in front of people, but when I came inside, she would say, "Fine, fine, just come in and wash your hands and eat something. If someone shouts at you just silently come home." I asked if I should take my clothes off and bathe. My mother said, "No, no—just change your clothes so others will think we are living in accord with society." Inside the home she did not allow these customs of society but outside she went along with it.

S: **You said that your passion is to recognize people's special gifts and then let them go in their own direction. You said you used to have 'fire quality,' which was a burning for yourself, but now you have 'water quality' which allows you to be lifted by those around you and this fills you with joy. Tell me more about these feelings.**

Biswadeb: As I grew up, I knew we had to break this caste system and to change many things. I wanted to change everything at once. I had a fire force and a need to burn this, and a need to burn that!

I was lucky that I had so many people in my life who helped me. The turning point in my life was when I met Yoland Trevino, an organizational consultant working for the United Nations in India. When I met Yoland, I saw how she interpreted "my fire." She helped me understand how the world is so big and that conflicts with people are a normal thing. I started to embrace people with attentive listening and was able to understand their life, rather than try to take revenge for the injustice I saw. I used to say, "He is named an 'untouchable'! That is wrong, there must be something we can do!" I learned how to absorb these difficulties rather than just want to fight them head on.

Meeting Yoland helped me understand how to embrace conflict. She taught me that if I don't feel the pain of people, I can't change the pain of people. I learned to use "waterpower." When you dissolve something into water, the water takes it in. I started to not reject these bad situations but to accept them as a way of seeing how we can change them. That was the biggest changing point in my life.

Most people who go to western countries are impressed by the lavish life and the many seductions that attract a younger generation. In India, we grow up in a very different set up. There is an extreme cultural value not to focus on yourself but to give to others. In the U.S. there is an extreme where everything is focused on self. While it is good to identify as an independent human being, this focus should be spiritually guided. If the spiritual connection is lacking, then "the self" is all about me and my problems. In western countries you focus on pleasing yourself. You want to eat? It's easy, all the food is there for you. Life has no boundaries. I went to the west with the precondition in my mind that there are problems in all countries, so I was not so lost in the U.S.

S: **You were not distracted by typical U.S. values because you already knew a deeper meaning in life.**

Biswadeb: In the U.S. I had amazing experiences; I experienced the extremes of power and wealth, and I met so many influential people. Yoland was working in the White House, and she was given an award by Hillary Clinton. I witnessed that and met so many influential people.

I even went to Hollywood and met a lot of stars. People said, "He has a good face, he looks like Omar Sharif. Can you come to my studio to do a photo shoot to be a model." I went! These are the experiences that I had of another world.

S: You stayed true to yourself. Another gift of yours is your musical talent. Please tell me why you love being a musician and how music serves a higher purpose for humanity.

Biswadeb: Music transcends ideology, it is heart to heart. Music doesn't need words. With music I can blend into every local culture wherever it is. Other things have this power, but music gives me direct access to any culture.

When I was little, my father used to chant every evening. Disciples would play drums and people would encourage me to play drums. This inspired me to start taking lessons and an uncle said I should take more lessons and play with them. Any rigorous effort must have sacrifice. I sacrificed time away from my mother's love to make music my internal love. I think everyone must be nurtured by love—loving a human being or loving an instrument. Music has given me a loving way to be aligned with myself.

In the rainy season school was closed and I would have extra time. My father was working, and I did not like being with the caretaker. I got depressed and cried for my mother. The rain was so hard.

But when I started playing the tabla, I played for hours, and I would not miss my mother so badly. The first 3 years were difficult, but my uncle and others guided me to play. I grew my own deep love for tabla and after 2-3 years no one needed to tell me to practice. I would practice for myself sometimes 6 or 7 hours a day.

S: All that practice certainly helped you become an accomplished tabla player!

Biswadeb: In 1992 I founded Ektaan (One Tone) when I finished high school. The purpose of Ektaan was to create a bond with the 'untouchable' communities. The lowest level of 'untouchables' is the 'sweepers', who clean up garbage and excrement. My friend Raju was from that community.

In the 1980s I liked a very funny poet who wrote how he could bring people of all faiths together. He thought if he built a temple, people would come but decided it would bring Hindus but not Muslims. Then he thought maybe he would build a church, but decided a church would not bring different religions together either. Finally, he drew a picture of a toilet, and wrote, "I know that people of all faiths will come because all people have to come to this place." His funny writings influenced me so much.

Musicians are from all backgrounds and music brings people together. No one says they are Hindu or Muslim or Christian, they just call themselves musicians.

I asked Raju if he would come with us in a caravan to play music at a few shows. At first, he was hesitant. I saw how difficult it was being an 'untouchable' because he was so afraid to go into a temple, to touch me, a Brahman. It doesn't matter how much space we give to them; their sense of lowliness is so entrenched. I had to experience their pain, the fear and oppression in their eyes; then I could finally understand better.

But finally, Raju said yes, and we went to play on a school stage in a village. We were sitting next to one another. I was so thirsty. Then I looked at his bottle of water right next to me and I took his bottle and drank his water. That is the worst thing I could have done because I am a Brahman. I was afraid, but I could see how really terrified he was! He was so terrified that he couldn't continue to play. He was just looking down and not playing. When the song finished, I leaned toward him and asked him what is the problem?

He said, "Why did you drink the water from my bottle?" I said, "So what, it's ok." No one on the stage said anything. That was the moment that I knew that music has the power to break this deep barrier.

I invited him to my home. He had food with me, and we played together. He cried and told me no one would ever believe that I drank water from his bottle. As a Brahman I should never do that. "Well, it was water, and I was thirsty. It is ok you are not punished." After the performance, everyone was paid. He said, "I want to treat you now to eat with me." We sat together and drank and toasted from the same glass. I told him, "From my heart you are my buddy, you are my fellow musician, we are both musicians." He came to my home many times and I helped him with master tabla lessons since he didn't have the money to pay for them. We are making a documentary about our story.

S: **Even in cultures that haven't changed, there are sparks of transformation, shifts toward higher consciousness. Has your friendship over the years changed the thinking of the people around you?**

Biswadeb: I would not have dared to do this practice in local communities if I had not joined URI. Breaking this norm alone is risky. It is a pretty impossible task. When I was introduced to URI, I realized there was already a global platform talking about ending discrimination.

In 1998 musicians came together and we decided to join URI as a local interfaith group. Since then, many things have changed. Today, there are 500 musicians in our Ektaan network. None of us believe in caste and we practice our values. We are strong as a network; we have people at the government level that support us.

There is still prejudice and superstitions, especially in remote areas. Raju and I don't often play in the band because we are seniors and don't play professionally anymore but we are still connected. Even with the grand successes we have had, one of the biggest challenges is that Raju's community is still told that his children must clean the toilets.

One boy from Raju's neighborhood came by and I hugged him and told him I was a friend of his uncle's and played tabla with him. This young guy was so scared that I hugged him. I asked, "You are educated but still must you do this work?" He said, "Yes, even with my education, I must do the 'sweeping' duty or my mother and father will be punished." This still needs to change. This boy should be able to do whatever he wants to do.

S: In your role with URI, you work with people who strive to give their lives dignity and protect their birthright land. Share a story that stays in your heart about what you have learned?

Biswadeb: I met a renowned social activist in my country. In 1975 he was a soldier in the Indian army during a conflict with China. Many Indian soldiers' lives were lost on the border with China. He was a truck driver and carried the dead bodies of his colleagues. He would pick up the dead bodies—all army men. One day he was driving out of the mountains with the dead bodies. He handed them over to another battalion. He went to a little railway station and decided to commit suicide by jumping in front of a train.

In all Indian rail stations, there is a wheel display of books for sale. He looked at a book by Swami Vivekananda and read a line in the book, "The purpose of human life is to live for others." He decided not to jump in front of the high-speed train.

After his retirement he went back to that village. The village was drug addicted, alcoholic, children did not go to school. In 25 years, he transformed the whole village. In social development, 25 years is nothing! His name is Anna Hazare and he is still alive.

When I was a student of Environmental Science and Risk Management in Mumbai I did my internship in the village where he was working. I was astonished to see that this village was so advanced—they even had a public toilet! In India at that time there were no such thing as public toilets!

I asked him what is the one thing you want me to know. He asked me, "Boy—if you expect to see a full field of crops what is most important?" I said, "good fertile land, hard work, labor" ... to everything I said he said, "no." He told me,

> Think about the seed, the seed must be buried underneath. That seed
> is the leader that you do not see. If you want to see society change you
> must bury yourself, you cannot be seen. That is how you can get a full
> field. If the leader says, "I want to be seen, I want to be in the forefront,
> no crops will come out." The leader must go underneath, out of sight,
> to have something happen above the ground.

S: There is so much joy and vitality in that way of living, like a seed.

Biswadeb: Yes, exactly. You must know that about yourself. This mantra gave me such perspective. I realized that I didn't care about people's recognition of the good things about me.

If I want other people to really come up as community leaders, I must go underneath. I want to be with people in this way. I want to be a channel of change—by being a seed.

S: That is profound. Are there others who helped you along the way?

Biswadeb: Yes, I have a special memory. I was having a tough time in my personal life. Yoland had helped me for many months go through the documentation process to stay in the U.S. It was just 7 days before my immigration and naturalization hearing, and I decided not to go ahead with that plan, and I returned to India. I knew I was giving up a lot, but this is what happens in life.

I met a teacher of my father's who was more than 100 years old. She lived in a cave in the Himalayas. I went to meet her at 6 o'clock at dusk, but they told me that she had already left and would not come back until morning at 7 o'clock. I thought, "oh no, no, what can I do if she is not here." I decided just to sit for a minute in the temple.

This was so strong; the experience I was going through was hell. I sat in the temple, leaned down and started chanting. From the back I heard small footsteps, someone walking. Then in the shadows, I saw this old lady dressed in ochre and I called to her, "Mataji." She came and hugged me, and she said, "I knew that you were coming, and I was waiting for your call." Believe me, that broke me into tears. It took me 10 minutes to come up and she told me, "everything is fine."

We sat and talked. The temple servants were so shocked. After 45 years she had never come back after she had gone to her cave. It was winter and already dark. She said, "I came because I wanted to see if you were calling me or not."

That was the moment when I had decided not to go to the hotel but just to sit and meditate. So often, we think that our prayer is not heard. It's not true, that moment changed me completely. Today, I strongly believe that when you sit down and pray wholeheartedly, your prayer gets heard.

S: **Thank you, your words are hitting me in a personal and powerful way.**

Biswadeb: Many times, we want our own version of the answer to our prayer. We pray but we don't see what we prayed for happen. Like when a teacher asks children if they see the red color, the children are so busy looking for the red color that they miss the white, green and other colors because they are busy looking for the red. What you look for in life, life will give you that.

My father used to tell me, "Don't be so persistent to do the one thing. God has given you karma in life. If you force something it might happen, but it might not be meant for you and will give you problems." I don't repent for anything. If want to buy a new car and if it does not happen, I know that it was not meant for me.

S: **How do you see the impact of your leadership with the different groups who are striving to improve their lives or bring up their community? What is it about you that helps them?**

Biswadeb: Being with people with full faith, believing that they can change things. It can be in our body language. When you stand in absolute surrender with pure love and commitment in the moment. When you stand in solidarity with people you see a change in their behavior. That is the first light of change; this is what Gandhi did.

That surrender in compassion is what influences me and I try to do that when I go to the communities. It is so important practically that we stand in solidarity with people. We speculate and judge so much. But it's not good to judge because we might not see the whole picture.

A spiritual teacher told me this story: "You see the lady fanning on the tomb of her dead husband? Do you know why? What would you say? She has gone mad, she is fanning her husband out of love." She is standing on the tomb fanning and people had all kinds of reasons why she was doing that, but no one knew until one man sat next to her in solidarity and simply asked, "What are you doing?" She said that she fell in love with a younger man. She told her husband that she would leave him to marry that man, and her husband was so upset that he had a heart attack. She rushed to her husband, and he held her hand and said, "Promise me that you will not marry that man until the dirt of my tomb dries." She is fanning so that dirt can dry quickly so she can marry the man.

S: Goodness, that's not what I expected to hear! We can never know until we stand with a person in solidarity.

Biswadeb: Our eyes see but still we don't know what's going on. There are things happening beyond what we pick up with our senses. If I see an action with my eyes and think I know what is happening, there still may be other things that I cannot see.

S: I remember you organized a food distribution project with villagers during Covid times. Instead of just giving food basket "handouts," you paired the villagers from different backgrounds so that each person was both a giver and a receiver.

Biswadeb: Even today, years after that project, the Muslim man who took a food basket to the Hindu family is still a brotherly friend to them. Now the Hindu family always calls him, and they go places together. Just experiencing a tiny spark of something good, people love it. All people want to be happy and peaceful. No one wants difficulties. The moment they feel happiness and beauty of life, they want to sustain it. It can be a relationship, a home, or even a small chair that you love. You want to keep hold of it.

As a catalytic force, we need to help people release bad practices and allow for good things to be sustained. It is not about me doing it for them; people must sustain these practices for themselves.

Even in my family, I was able to change things. I asked my family to write a list of their best friends. "Be honest," I said. "Sit down and think of who your 10 best friends are. If you see that no one is from a different religion, then your life is not enriched and as interesting as it could be.

You are just staying within your own community. India is a home of great religions: Buddhism, Sikhism, Hinduism, Islam, Christianity. If you do not have at least one person out of 10 on your list, go back and change something in your life. Instead of blaming a Muslim, blaming a Christian, make yourself available to them and put yourself in their shoes. It will only happen when you have a friend from a different faith tradition."

I am doing this for every family member these days. I tell them, "You want to give me a gift? Give me the gift that you are friends with a person from a different religion."

S: Are you witnessing people increasing their capacity to treat one another with respect and compassion?

Biswadeb: I work as an interfaith peace builder but I don't believe that religions have a strong enough power to bring people to a higher level. They don't. They can't. The darkness we are going through is not a dying but a birthing. I believe what Valerie Kaur says, "This darkness is the womb, not the tomb."

The younger generation in India is motivated toward spirituality which is the greatest hope. They understand spirituality and they don't want it to be mixed up with traditional religion.

For me, this is hope because spirituality gives strong guidance, it gives a sense of Oneness. It is believing that every living thing matters on this Earth, everything is part of the Whole. In Hinduism there is a saying, "Each of us is the son of Oneness." That is what the younger generation is recognizing. They have seen enough wars now, enough loss of life, enough conflicts. They are not going to be more religious. I think religions have boundaries that cannot be crossed. Scholars have beautified the teachings of religions but that is not enough. Religious differences separate people and provoke them to kill each other. Spirituality offers a Oneness that is different.

S: I see a global heart of democracy arising where people are taking up responsibility for the wellbeing of the global community. What do you see?

Biswadeb: To me, another understanding of 'global heart' is the African phrase Ubuntu. "I am because you are. You think about me, I think about you." Even when I drive, I look around me now to see how I can move to give the other guy more space. Yes, I see the sense of Ubuntu growing.

When this sense grows, I see the global heart. When we evolve from "me to we," we accept the global heart. I believe that this is what the next energy wave is bringing to all of us.

S: **I'm so eager to learn about people who are living from this "global heart." As we are nearing the end of our conversation, is there something you would like to add?**

Biswadeb: I always tell people that whenever we practice anything it should engage all our senses. Our five senses are there to give us the utmost physical experience in Oneness, affection and solidarity. When you meditate you close your eyes and focus on quieting the mind. I like music and sports because we are not only centered and focused, but we use all our senses, all our organs.

I call it music. When I drum, I receive the rhythm. I feel the rhythm, I recite the rhythm. It is a complete inclusive engagement. That is a true transformation.

People should practice anything physically integrating like running, drumming and all kinds of music. This supports internal as well as external transformation. We must engage both or there could be a imbalance. Our bodies may want something but our hearts want something else. I learned from my father that this alignment is called 'tantra.' In India ancient 'tantra' teaches that internal wisdom must align with our physical body.

If you meet a guru, you see that their body language is fixed. They helped me learn how to see the forms in the formless and to see the formless in the form. When I only saw the form of a deity in the Hindu religion my father said, "you are stuck in the form. You must go beyond the form to understand the formless. You see into the formless and your eyes can draw forth the form. It is you that is creating the form."

S: **So, maybe we don't need to retreat from society to be spiritual, we can embody the spiritual and give it form through our actions.**

Biswadeb: Exactly. Embodiment is very important. We have our human body; our body will teach us how to embody the formless.

S: **Thank you Biswadeb for the spiritual truths that you hold and share in this conversation.**

Biswadeb: Working with you over the years has been a channel of peace and joy for all of us. Ubuntu is you and me, and me and you and that we are that joy together. Your presence is always blissful. Having people like you in my life gives me joy.

S: Yes, there is a joy we are both embodying and experiencing together right now!

To me, another understanding of 'global heart' is the African phrase Ubuntu. "I am because you are. You think about me, I think about you."

About Biswadeb

Biswadeb holds a bachelor's degree in accounting and masters in business administration. He has served as Coordinator for URI Asia East India for 23 years and lives with his wife and daughter in Kolkata, India. In his role with URI, Biswadeb directs a staff team who serves as the "wind beneath the wings" of many local community development initiatives, including the work of Adivasi tribal members to receive legal rights to their ancestral lands.

During a recent URI assembly of local interfaith groups in East India, Biswadeb gave voice to his lifelong calling: "may the diversity of peoples make the land of peace fertile as we stand in gratitude co-creating a stronger platform of mutual understanding." Biswadeb lights up when he witnesses people using their own initiatives and talents to make their lives better. He says, "Staying close to the people in the village communities helps me stay pure and know in my heart that we shall overcome."

I realized that I didn't care about people's recognition of the good things about me. If I want these other people to really come up as community leaders, I must go underneath. I want to be with people in this way. I want to be a channel of change—by being a seed.

Elisabeth Ziegler-Duregger

Elisabeth raises the meaning of the phrase an "ordinary person who does extraordinary things" to the next level!

I do everything from the kitchen table.

Although I had heard about Elisabeth's work supporting refugee camps in Syria, I understood her exceptional life better when we both turned up every Friday in the last few years to join an online Global Prayer Gathering. Elisabeth joins the gathering while sitting at her kitchen table, in reverent stillness offering simple prayers for peace and deep assurance in the ultimate power of Divine Love moving humanity toward experiencing Heaven on Earth.

Recently, Elisabeth engaged me in "making the impossible possible" with the idea of an "International Law of Personal Responsibility." The law, applicable to people all over the world, would require every person to take an oath of personal responsibility to make reparation to the families for every life he or she takes (in wars or not) or any damage to land and property he or she causes. Letting go of that visionary idea, she had to rush to her hometown's Christmas Market to raise money for practical needs of women and children in Syrian refugee camps. A local group of volunteers, Education Brings Peace, was selling tickets to help people in the camps: 5 Euros = 50 bowls of soup, a warm tent for 2 weeks, or one fig tree for the future."

Elisabeth's family farmhouse dates back 800 years in East Tyrol Austria. Names from the ancestors have been known since 1545. Her identity is deeply rooted in her homeplace, with memories of working with the horse in the fields as a child. With roots as a local farm girl, Elisabeth's identity has expanded widely to see herself as a global citizen. She "walks with" people who endure hardship, offers loving friendship and helps them find solutions to their problems.

S: I've been exploring how ordinary people act from their deepest spiritual values and intentions to serve, in their families, communities and the world. I'm gathering stories of people who are doing what I call guiding light work for all of us. When I was in Austria, I observed that you have contributed most of your life by seeing problems and solutions and living into new possibilities by bringing along your community. I am curious to learn more about you, to learn about your childhood in Lienz, the small town where you grew up, and what you valued most in your upbringing.

Elisabeth: My kind of living has a long history. The stories I hear about my grandparents are all about helping others. So, it is a core value of our family to serve others without getting money. Money was never a focus in our farmer's family. In former days people here were very poor, they just survived with things they produced on the farm. They told me that besides sugar and coffee they didn't buy anything. They did a lot of work.

My grandmother and grandfather tried their best to help refugees in 1945. I was raised in town, about 4 kilometers from our family farm, by my grand-aunt and great grandparents. My great grandparents had experienced two world wars. My great grandfather was born in 1874 and died at age 100 in 1974. I was 19 years old when he died and learned a lot from his life experience.

I'm a very curious person and like to invent things — social things. If I come across a problem I say, "Here's a problem, what can we do?" My brain is like this, it likes to look at problems and think of solutions that we can do something about.

S: How did that come about? Were you like that as a child?

Elisabeth: When I look back, I see that I was a very bad pupil. If you look at my grades, they were very bad. If I didn't see the meaning in what I was learning I refused to learn anything. I didn't learn Latin. I just learned enough not to be thrown out of the school. I never valued having good grades.

S: What were you searching for that made you impatient?

Elisabeth: To get active I need an aim, an emotional aim. Just working with numbers on a paper was not an aim for me. The same happened to me at the university. I started at the age of 35 and I already had my family and started part time. If they couldn't tell me why I should read this book or write this paper, I refused.

S: Sounds like you were stubborn not because you didn't want to learn but because you wanted your learning to have meaning for you. Do you remember when you began to get active about something that did have meaning for you?

Elisabeth: During my younger school years until 18, I was an ordinary schoolgirl. During the holidays I had to help on the farm and didn't have time. But just 2 weeks after finishing my school at 19, I started working in the town library. Then my creative 'juices' started quickly to flow. I helped the founder of the library make new floors and renovate the space. I designed new furniture for the library because the old looked so boring. I decided there should be new furniture.

I had the great privilege of having a boss who was sure that all the things I did were for the best for the library, so I could invent things and do what I liked. He knew I was a bit crazy but in a good way, not in a dangerous way for the library. His name was Pater Basilius, a Franciscan monk. He was born in 1919 and was from a refugee family from the former Yugoslavia.

It was a blessing for me that during my professional life that lasted until I was 59, I could always solve problems that had meaning for me.

S: You have a keen sense of what is needed and did not accept the status quo. And, then there is also your amazing creativity. People may have an idea, but to bring that idea into form is a special talent. What intention did you have for the library? How did you want people to feel when they came to the library?

Elisabeth: I always wanted people to leave the library happier than they came. Because the library was in a Catholic monastery, we had a good safe space for people to talk about their deepest sorrows. I liked to listen to them, whether children or old people, people felt very much at home there. When I meet former library visitors, they tell me they miss the small old library for emotional reasons. The new library is modern, but we were able to do something different. I don't think people go to the new library to tell the staff that they are sad and that they are mourning the loss of somebody. This was one of my talents that I always loved people (not always but most of the time (laughs)).

I was able to act in another way than the way librarians must work now. Now, librarians are caught up with rules and must reach special numbers to receive funding.

S: **You really did offer something to people that way beyond books. How did this happen?**

Elisabeth: After working in the library for fourteen years we started to work with computers. We had the third most advanced internet access in the whole region because my boss was very much involved in technology. I thought, "With this advanced computer technology what information do people here need to help them live their lives?"

First, I thought they need something to eat. So, we collected information about what the local farmers were producing. Then I was interested in all the talents of the people in the area. I collected names of people who make music, write books, who had special talents and services to offer.

I made a list of people living in the region who came from other countries. We started a program to help women from foreign countries who married local men. And sometimes they couldn't talk about how bad their lives were, so we listened to them, and there were others who left their home countries and we formed a new kind of family for them.

I tried to change the mind of our people here against foreigners. We gave them a new name and did not call them foreigners but "Cultural Ambassadors."

S: **That's brilliant!**

Elisabeth: We honored them with a ceremony and presented them with a certificate that included the sentence, "With your special talents, knowledge and contacts you are a gift for our region. We ask you to make good connections between East Tyrol and your home country." People liked not being a foreigner but a Cultural Ambassador.

S: **How did that program work out?**

Elisabeth: We started with this program in 1995 and had a nice cultural meeting each year for many years.

In 2004 the municipal government in Lienz decided to establish a Refugee House here. Nobody spoke against it. I'm sure that this work that gave people from other countries official value paid off over the years.

We invited refugees to stay in the center of the town rather than in the mountains where no one can see them. They stayed in town at a well-organized Refugee House. Over the years, the people here changed their view of foreigners.

In the meantime, it also got more challenging because most of the new refugees were Muslims. Just yesterday I spoke to our adult education center that I want to have more educational programs about Islam and other religions, even more than we have done until now. There is a lot more work to do. There are young people who are not aware of the programs from a long time ago. We must start again for the new generations.

S: **Where do you think the motivation came from inside yourself to do these things—to know that it was important to listen to people who had loss and pain, and to be a culture breaker in welcoming the stranger as a gift?**

Elisabeth: The value about different religions and cultures came from the books that I read when I was young. There was a German author, Karl May. I also loved learning about Native Americans!

The part of my work with people who were mourning came from my family. My mother had 10 children and 5 died. I've always liked to be with dying people and I have no fear. It is life knowledge and book knowledge that has made me who I am. Some talents I got from … somewhere … maybe over the rainbow (laughs).

S: **Let's look at "over the rainbow." You mentioned that you live in a place where you can see beyond the next high horizon. There is a mountain range, and you can see beyond it to another mountain range. How has that geography helped to shape you?**

Elisabeth: I feel very cozy here. Our town is a good place. The mountains are around us and I feel that they keep me safe. They are not so narrow that I feel limited. I feel protected here. I feel different when I go to Vienna by train and come to the area where everything is flat. I feel very strong in this landscape. Here, I am often on top of a mountain and my eyes have a wider horizon. Even when I am sitting at my kitchen table praying with people from all over the world my heart has no boundaries.

S: **Your high-altitude view and your kitchen table help you feel a part of the fabric of global connectedness.**

Elisabeth: I am happy to see the stars. We really can watch the stars here. This evening, I saw Jupiter just above me. Then, I always feel that the whole universe is all around me. It is a special feeling to be a little grain of sand in this universe.

S: **How does this influence you?**

Elisabeth: It gives me a feeling of responsibility. When I see all that has been given to this planet it makes me feel responsible for the whole planet as far as I can reach or as far as my ideas can reach.

Of course, I must mention my Catholic upbringing and my love for people in the Catholic Church.

S: **Tell me about this. So many people don't go to church anymore.**

Elisabeth: In our region, the people are very grounded in religion. Not just in a talking way or a fearful way but in an active, loving, authentic way. I don't go to Mass on Sunday very often. But our priest knows that the parish can count on my help at any time. I am very comfortable at home on Sundays. They know that I am a person who will work with them any time they ask me.

S: **Is there a special teaching from Catholicism or from Jesus' teaching that you hold close to your heart?**

Elisabeth: Yes, I was in Jerusalem with an exchange program in my early 20s. I walked to Golgotha, the place of the crucifixion of Jesus. I sat there and waited for a great miracle to happen to me (laughs). I sat under an olive tree waiting but nothing happened. But I had a Bible with me and opened it. I saw two sentences that I follow now.

Jesus said, "I came so that you have a good life, a life of fullness—that is the reason that I came to this Earth." So, I understood that there is an aim that we all have a good life.

I read another sentence that went something like, "For people who honor God everything in life will turn out good." That is my life experience. Have a good life and don't be afraid. Don't be afraid and have a good life. That is a good summary of my life.

S: **Thank you, that is very good. I know that there is a series of books called The Little Owl that is important in your work. Can you tell me about it?**

Elisabeth: The author of this story, Lene Mayer-Skumanz, came to our library to read these books in 1998. It was just two months before Austria became a leading member in the European Union (EU). When I heard this story, I thought this is very similar to the problems of the EU because every country thinks they are the most important one and they know best what to do and how to live.

We asked the Cultural Ambassadors in the region to translate this story in their mother tongue and used the internet to send it as a present to the EU Presidency in Austria. We asked them to send it to the member countries of the EU as a gift for their libraries.

The story is about a little owl who was sent out into the world to get wisdom by her parents. The little owl said, "I am so small. How can I do this?" The parents answered, "The Great Owl who created everything will take care of you."

The little owl comes across different animals, and they say it is good that you came along because owls know the answers to all the questions of the world. Each one had a special question for the little owl. A bat asked, "Why did the Great Bat who created everything allow that I have just one child and no more?" A peacock asked, "Why did the Great Peacock who created everything make only one tree where there is enough space for my big tail?" A wild cat asked, "Why did the Great Wild Cat that created everything allow that there are cats that allow to be touched."

The owl went to a house in the woods where she met a woman who was singing and the owl asked her, "Why are you singing?" The woman said, "I am singing to honor the Great Mother who created everything." Little owl asked, "Where is she?" The woman answered, "She is everywhere, and the stars are her jewelry on her garments."

The owl went far into the woods and found a house with an old man inside. Little owl asked the old man what he was doing. The man said, "I am reading a book about the Great Father who created everything." The little owl said, "I am confused because the peacock thought it was the Great Peacock that had created everything, the bat thought it was the Great Bat, the woman said the Great Mother has created everything. These butterflies will think that the Great Butterfly has created everything." The old man answered, "They cannot imagine anything else."

When the owl was in the wood, she saw a little child sitting quietly with a cat on her lap. The owl asked herself, "I wonder what name the child will give to 'the Great Secret' that created everything." The owl realized that the child doesn't need to call it by name because the child is sitting in the full presence of it.

Then the little owl went back to her parents. Her father asked,"Did the Great Owl who created everything allow you to find wisdom?" The little owl said, "Yes, now I am very wise and now I will tell everyone what I found." Father said, "My child, that is a good plan, but it is only with people that you will have problems. They do not believe us."

This is a very nice story. You can use it in many ways with children and adults. It is a good tool for interreligious work, and intercultural work. Translators came from different religions and countries to help spread the book to different places.

S: **How did this book connect you with the camps in Syria?**

Elisabeth: When I heard that there was a man running refugee camps in Syria for women and children, I sent him this book and this is what started my connection with Hasan Abo Ali, the director of these camps.

S: **Please tell me more about how you and your group in Lienz are supporting these camps?**

Elisabeth: I think it is a gift from heaven that we met. Hasan always tells me that when we first met, he was in a very bad personal situation. His father had died. He couldn't get any help from the people he was trying to care for. He said that I came into his life through the story of "The Little Owl." After these conversations he said that he started to see more light on the horizon. Of course, we started to send money to buy necessary things for the camp like food and many other things.

We communicate via WhatsApp so he can translate from English to Arabic. He studied English as part of his education at the Electro-Technic University in Syria. He said that the years of war had made him lose much of his English, but he is learning again and improving.

He dreams about helping people all over the world. Just yesterday he wrote that he wants to offer his skills to people in other countries. He believes that someday there will be peace in Syria, and he can leave knowing that people are self-sustaining there so he can go other places. He would also like to write books on the history of Syria. He found a lot of artifacts around Camp Mariam.

S: **How did your relationship grow? It is so much more than just a fund-raising service project for you and the people of Lienz.**

Elisabeth: Hasan and I came into direct contact in February 2022. Since that first day, we talk about one hour every night between midnight and 1 am. During the day he must work, but during the night we make plans, and he tells me what is happening.

Recently, there have been very heavy bombings near the camps. Every morning, he sends me a message, "we are still alive." Then, we start thinking about what is our next problem to solve and we talk about our dreams.

It is Hasan's dream to build a place of prayer for people from all religions in this area of Syria. When peace returns here one day, tourists from all over the world will come to visit and it can be like it was before the war.

My dream is to bring together groups of women in Syria under the name "Little Sisters of Mariam" and at the same time to bring together Christian women in Austria. Jesus is called Prophet Isa in Islam and Mary is called Mariam. The women can share strong support and learn how Mary and Mariam are revered in both Christianity and Islam. People here are not aware of this, and this causes a lot of wrong ideas about Islam. It would be wonderful to write prayers with both groups. They come from different ways of life, but one heart. My dream is that they come together in "Mariam's Heart."

S: **This reminds me of your mountain after mountain landscape. Once you meet one problem or circumstance that needs help, there is another "horizon" or issue that needs solving to move towards. How does this project in Syria affect your community in Lienz?**

Elisabeth: Most of our people are very open. About 45,000 people live in East Tyrol and I think they are special people. When you go just 30 kilometers away to South Tyrol, the people there have other values, and they are much more focused on money. Here in our surroundings, having a lot of money is not the biggest value people are thinking about.

A few years ago, I spoke to a Muslim man about money at the Parliament of the World's Religions. He said in the U.S. many people think that God loves them if they have a lot of money. I told him in our surroundings it is different. People think that maybe a person with a lot of money is working with the devil. In our minds he wouldn't have money unless he was working with "the dark side." Here it is more valuable to give things away and help people than it is to have a big bank account. This culture makes it easy for me to collect money and I have lots of good ideas about how to raise it. I tell them that they will receive a lot of blessings.

S: **I see how creative you are in developing ways to raise money. Have people in your group changed because of their relationship to the refugee camps?**

Elisabeth: I'm so happy that I'm able to send photos of what is happening at the camps to our local WhatsApp list, and I put news on the group's website. People here feel close to the life there. I try to talk about the balance … yes, there are many problems and many solutions have been achieved. That way they are not overthrown with just the problems.

They like that they know where the money goes. There are big organizations where you don't know how much of the money you give goes to the people who need it, etc. In Lienz, the people know that everything they give is going to help the kids in need. This makes it a lot easier to ask them for money. And, I don't have an office, I do everything from the kitchen table.

Elisabeth: At the camps there are women, children and old people. Only in one camp there are some men because 20 families came who were displaced after the earthquake. There are 16 children there who are orphans. Most of the children are half orphans because they only have a mother or a grandmother. There is no one to teach the children because the mothers were not allowed to learn how to read and write.

S: **It seems like a miracle that there in that desert land, the farming work that Hasan leads is creating an abundance of fruits and vegetables. How is that happening?**

Elisabeth: If you ask him his answer is, "Chicken manure and the friendship from Austria is my fertilizer."

Of course, the problem there is having enough water. He uses strip irrigation and tries new methods of agriculture. He had never planted anything before he started learning how to farm at the camps last year.

The first thing we gave him was money to buy boxes to plant flowers, so the people had something beautiful to see and that would put other thoughts in their minds. We also gave soccer balls and dolls for the children and sweets. This was the start … these flower boxes.

In the meantime, he has kept growing gardens. Nearly every family has their own garden and there are big community gardens that grow a lot of food. Hasan picks the vegetables and gives them to families, and he makes sure that each family gets the same amount, so no one is jealous. He is very careful about this.

S: **You two are a perfect match! Hasan has endless needs and problems to solve, and you are an energetic, resourceful problem solver.**

Elisabeth: Yes, I spoke about this with him. I read a book when I was 20, called *I Want to Green the Desert*. Now, that desire is true for me. Hasan has the desert, and I am helping to green it.

Here in Lienz, we are looking to bring the dreams of people together with the dreams of people in other places. We are looking at how to match people's dreams. This makes me happy. I almost feel guilty because Hasan's problems give me the chance to fulfill my dreams.

S: **As forerunners showing what's possible, you two are modeling how the dreams of people can match up together. We might call it serendipity, a miracle or God's grace, but your relationship with Hasan makes it clear that together you both are finding endless ways to help each other live your dreams.**

Elisabeth: And it makes me so happy! I can do the things that I like. My brain likes to think about solutions. If everything is ok, what would I think about? My life would be rather boring! I really hope that when I die and I hope to be in heaven, that there is something left to do there for me.

S: **There is another big idea of yours I want to touch on. You said that the Bell of Peace and Friendship was a project to relate to violence in the world. Please say more about that dream.**

Elisabeth: This idea was born to make a balance with a very sad event in our history here. In 1945, 25,000 refugees, Cossacks from Russia and Ukraine, came to our valley. There were 38,000 inhabitants at that time and 25,000 refugees so you can imagine the problems that this situation brought.

These refugees were looking for a new place to live because they did not want to go back to Russia where they had been persecuted by the Bolsheviks and Stalin. They had fought on the side of the Germans because Hitler had promised them a new place to live.

At this time after the war, the British soldiers were occupying this area. The soldiers planned to send the refugees back to Russia as a swap for the release of British soldiers who were prisoners of war. In Russia's view they had been enemies working with Hitler. Ninety-five percent went to Siberia and died.

The Cossacks knew that they would be killed when they were sent back to Russia. Many committed suicide here. Many threw themselves into the river and died. The Cossack soldiers had their families with them, with wagons, horses, children and women. Some mothers threw their babies in the water or jumped into the river with their babies. I know about one mother who gave her child to another woman to take care of and threw herself in the water. Just the child survived.

This history is very hard. People here who were sensitive saw that this history was like a dark fog—they could see this cloud of death and fear all over the valley even 50 years later.

Every year there is a ceremony here to remember this tragedy. In 2005, I was at the cemetery where some of the graves are. I thought, "Let us take the energy of this sad history and change it to a positive energy." We can use this "bad soil" and transform it so that something good and healthy grows for our area and for the world. The initial idea was to bring forth a balance with what had happened.

First, I wanted to build a church there on the mountain, but it wasn't allowed. I got the idea to build a bell tower. It took 10 years but now the bell for Peace and Friendship is there on the mountain. People from other countries brought stones to place around the bell. I think it is a perfect match, a bell surrounded by stones from many countries of the world and from the holy places of different religions like Mecca, Lhasa, the river Ganga, Rome, Assisi, Stonehenge and many more.

I was inspired by the World Peace Prayer Society's Peace Pole project and the words, "May Peace Prevail on Earth," but I chose the words, "May Peace and Friendship Prevail on Earth," because I think only peace is not enough. For me, the ability for people to be together in friendship is more important to me than only having peace.

S: The bell is a remarkable and uplifting symbol and to hear its ringing vibration on the mountain is powerful. When you hear this ringing vibration what do you imagine is happening?

Elisabeth: When I watch people ringing the bell, children especially like to ring it. I think that they get an impulse to think about what the words "friendship" and "peace" mean.

Some don't care about religion, but they like to see the stones from all over the world and to see how similar these stones look. If a stone doesn't have a sign from a certain country, it's easy to imagine how these stones could be from anywhere in the world. This is an underlying message of this place. Just as stones are similar from all over the world, people from all over the world also are similar in their feelings and fears. To touch the stones is a special feeling.

S: Yes, this is a grounded way people can see we are all connected. I read that inscribed on the bell tower are the words, "May there be Heaven on Earth everywhere."

Elisabeth: I put this sentence on the bell tower this year. It takes more than peace and friendship to have a good life for all. It takes healed nature; it takes a just economy; of course, it takes good government to bring all the other things. Heaven on Earth is the "meta" space—above all other wishes people can have.

To have a good family is heaven on Earth, to live with healthy nature is heaven on Earth, to live in peace is heaven on Earth. To have all creation, people, animals and plants healthy—each is a little part—together it can be heaven on Earth, but we need to work on it.

S: Do you see people working on it? What green shoots do you see growing now? Is it possible for there to be this kind of heaven on Earth?

Elisabeth: Yes, it is possible. I started collecting names of good projects some years ago, but I had to stop this work because there are so many good people working in all areas, I couldn't keep up. If I lived 100 years more, I could never count all the good projects!

Just before we started our talk, I found a project in Australia where people are creating gardens and enriching biodiversity. People in every country are working on the right things. The media cannot keep up and cover all of this.

S: What do you think is motivating people to do this good work? This impulse and action are what I call the heart of democracy. People have a natural inclination to see a need and reach out to do good. How do you explain that?

Elisabeth: When we start our life, babies are very open at birth. Even at two years old, babies want to help. Then things happen in their life that puts stones on their souls. Some survive this and keep their heart open.

It is not so much the situation of hunger or war or other problems if they are surrounded with love. Babies endure a lot of problems. They can be rich in material things and have no love that makes them feel safe and good. Then, they have a difficult road through their lives and try to fill the hole in their hearts with material things around them.

Hasan tries to give the children the good feeling that they have survived a bad situation. Yesterday, he wrote that he wants to put love in their hearts, love for animals and love for flowers.

So, we bought some good food for the birds. The war took away the birds and they have no birds. We bought bird food so that the birds would come back.

It is a big aim of Hasan's to help the children and nurture their good feelings by playing with animals and tending to plants. For the earthquake victims, he made a flower garden down the center of their row of tents. Just to feed their souls with flowers. He cannot feed them with music now, but he plans to buy a guitar and feed them with music too. Everything that brings joy to their heart will help to make them good people. This is his aim.

From my own family I learned that if you are raised with love then you have a lot of power to survive different situations. I had a good situation growing up and I can use this power to help others in a bad situation. Even more than feeding bodies, it is important to feed the heart.

S: **Yes, giving attention to the loving part of us as human beings is important. The human heart is central to experiencing heaven on Earth.**

Elisabeth: This can happen at any age. I am working in a residency for elderly people. For many years I have been going there and putting pictures on their walls with poems. Just to bring new thoughts to their minds. I see how happy they are when they can do something active and positive for the world. This longing is so deep in our minds and bodies, whatever you call it. The wish that all live the reality of Heaven on Earth is the core in people, maybe in every animal as well.

There are layers of bad experiences and false values with advertising and even with religion that overtake our minds. These other values can be read even in the Holy Books, about killing and vengeance against the enemy. These wrong ideas are like a black layer on top of the colorful soul that lies underneath.

S: **I love that you said that inside of us is an intent for all beings to live in Heaven on Earth. That intention inside of us makes it possible.**

Elisabeth. When somebody sees another doing something good, it is easier for them to do good as well. I think that is the strength of the

United Religions Initiative—that people are connected and reinforced by others doing good work.

I read a book some years ago, *Catalogue of Hope*. It was at a time when the media was full of all the problems of the world. I nearly lost hope. Then I read this book that was just a collection of good ideas and good projects. This changed my mind and my feelings. I didn't think that I am too small, problems are too big, I am helpless. In this book I saw a person working on this problem, another working on another problem. This book was a game changer for me.

S: **People to people share their ideas and projects. Seeing one another doing good work and being lifted by the work of others.**

Elisabeth: Not everyone has the chance to take on such a playground as Hasan's camps. Just to go through town a with a smile on your face is a start. It seems so little and so easy, but it's not done. Here, in our surroundings everyone should smile. We have the duty to smile here!

S: **This is a good place to draw our wonderful conversation to a close. You said that it all begins with a smile on your face. Is there anything else that you want to share with people about what is important to pay attention to?**

Elisabeth: My answer sounds so esoteric—focus on love. It's more important than the critical thinking that we have been taught in school. Today, I thought that if I were to become a politician I would go to every town and invite the people to try and come up with better ideas to solve the problems. They are only allowed to come if they have a better idea. During the last 30 years, education focused on how to analyze and be critical about everything. The next step must be to take over responsibility.

S: **As you said, it's not heavy to take on responsibility, it's fun because it asks people to think creatively of a better idea.**

Elisabeth: Yes, it is so much better than watching soap operas. It is fun to think of solutions and creative ideas; this is what makes life so interesting. For me, it's like a playground, a worthwhile playground.

S: **You deepen the meaning of the word playground to mean a place where you enter a world where we say, "Let's try something and see what happens."**

Elisabeth: If you asked me five years ago, I don't know what I would answer about my future. I would never have thought that I would take over responsibility for 725 refugees! This opportunity to be with Hasan who is a match to my dreams, just showed up for me and is a gift to me.

S: It's an incredible gift for me to know you better and to be a witness to your life. There are so many people like you living from their heart.

Elisabeth: There are black areas still around. I think of what could have happened to Putin, Assad, Netanyahu, people who make such a lot of darkness in the world. What must have happened to them as a baby, to cut off all their feelings?

I feel the day that they die, and they open their eyes, and they see all the things that they did and the people who followed them, I'm sure they will be very sad about each crying child.

S: It is a somber note that we live in a world where evil and good are in constant tension. Do you have a last word about what gives you sustenance, especially in the face of evil?

Elisabeth: When people ask me how I stay positive, I say I have no time to think about bad things. I need my time to find a solution for the next thing to do. I need to figure out how to help Hasan keep the tents warm for the winter. This keeps my mind busy. I have no time for bad things.

S: Lots of wisdom there and lots of fulfillment. Hearts are meant to be fulfilled. We must ask, what does fulfill our heart? How do we take responsible action out of love?

Elisabeth: I have met so many people who I can love so I am very thankful for my life. For many years I was sad that not all my ideas were able to come to fruition. I watched the tree in my garden and realized that no one is blaming the tree and that not all its seeds are growing to be a big tree. I will not be blamed that not all my idea seeds will be a big success.

S: Yes, and just because the seeds didn't grow to be big trees doesn't mean the seeds didn't have meaning just as seeds.

Elisabeth: My brain likes to be asked questions and to have a reason to think about things. Your questions are a gift to me, and I am sure for others, too. It is important to do these interviews because people need to be asked and feel that another is listening to them.

S: With each interview I feel so happy, and I know this is what I am supposed to do.

About Elisabeth

Elisabeth was born in 1955, has been married for 39 years to a former army officer and has one son. Choosing to forego training as a medical technician that would take her to another part of Austria, at 19 years old and two weeks after finishing at her local secondary school, Elisabeth took a job as the librarian at the town library. Her job provided freedom to innovate exciting changes at the library and tackle local community needs. She remained the town's favorite librarian for 35 years.

Experiencing deaths in her own family, Elisabeth felt drawn to accompany others in their losses. For more than 15 years she has supported townspeople in their grief and led memorial services. Elisabeth's conviction that "death is a gateway to a reality filled with love … and God is very close and holds everything together," inspired her to write several books of poetry and meditative prayers, including *Solace of the Mountains, Accompaniment on Paths of Grief* and *On the Way to Another Life. Meditative Texts for Hospice Work and Grief Support.*

In 2022, "Roots of Friendship, Mariam Meets Maria," a project in Syria organized by the local interfaith group co-founded by Elisabeth, received a World Interfaith Harmony Week prize, awarded by the United Nations.

Night after night from 12midnight to 2am, Elisabeth confers online with Hasan Abo Ali, director of the camps in Syria. They share dreams and resolve problems. They are proving that "the wave of friendship is stronger than the destruction caused by people and nature."

Today, I thought that if I were to become a politician I would go to every town and invite the people to try and come up with better ideas to solve problems. They are only allowed to come if they have a better idea. During the last 30 years, education focused on how to analyze and be critical about everything. The next step must be to take over responsibility.

Hasan Abo Ali

I always feel that I am like a seed. This seed must grow wherever it is planted and give good crops and results. I see that whoever does not have goodness in the land in which he lives will have no goodness in any place he goes.

His prayers expand way beyond his present dangerous and harsh conditions …

Hasan is a regular participant in a Global Prayer Gathering that has been meeting every week for over three years. He appears on the Zoom screen … looking straight into our hearts, vulnerable, earnest, solid, humbly present. In the background we can hear children's voices from the Mariam Refugee Camp in Syria. When Hasan does not appear on the screen, we wonder if bombs have struck in the night, we wonder if he and the hundreds of people in these camps are still alive and unharmed. When Hasan offers prayers, he prays for people in the world to be free from suffering, for criminals to stop killing, for people in every country to live in peace and prosperity. I am in awe that his prayers expand way beyond his present dangerous and harsh conditions and faithfully seek the wellbeing of people everywhere.

Hasan was invited to join the global prayer group by Elisabeth Ziegler Duregger, his soulmate and good friend whom he describes as "more than human," his "angel" with whom he creates, colludes and churns out ideas to transform danger and misery into life-giving solutions for the people in the refugee camps. Elisabeth and Hasan may never win the Nobel Peace Prize but their fervor to find solutions that empower life, primarily for mothers and children whose lives have been torn apart by endless war, is incomparable.

Where does the strength that sustains their faith, their creative problem solving come from? How do they refuel their dreams and those of the people they serve? Their hearts are alive with love for God, for one another, for the children, for the highest outcomes for humanity. More than the acres of vegetable gardens, Hasan, Elisabeth and all who participate are seeding gardens of "people power" for generations to come.

S: **Please share experiences from your upbringing that are important to you and that guided you to be the person you are today.**

Hasan: I was born and raised in the city of Aleppo, Syria and I had many experiences there. My father loved me and wanted me to be different from what my mother wanted. My father was different from everyone else and from the beginning of my life, he wanted me to be like him. Many accused him of being a Freemason because of his ideas. In the past in Aleppo society, anyone who had tolerant ideas, open with love to the world, was called a Freemason, even though many people did not know the meaning of Freemasonry.

My mother wanted me to study Islamic sciences and become a sheikh, while my father wanted me to become a politician or an intelligence officer. He and my mother were opposites in thought and ideas. He used to tell me, "Don't grow a beard. I don't trust those who have a beard." He was referring to the perception that having a beard was needed to be an authentic Islamic scholar. He always defended the Jews and considered that the Ottomans had lost their founding principles and their identity.

When I was young, I had a dream while I was sleeping that still accompanies me to this day. I saw that I was praying in front of the Al-Buraq Al-Sharif Wall in Jerusalem, even though I knew nothing about it. At that time, while I was praying, a young Palestinian man came to me screaming, "Oh, Hasan," so I turned to him. He tried to shoot and kill me. I told my father about the dream, and he told me, "There will come a day when you will go to Israel and pray there."

S: **I hope one day you will pray there and be safe. Please say more about how you came to embrace tolerance and respect for all religions.**

Hasan: My father did not like religious extremism, and he instilled tolerance in me from a young age. We are all brothers, and our souls and the souls of our ancestors for thousands of years are one soul. I always feel the power of ancestors and spirits within me.

Before the war, whenever I entered an ancient archaeological site, I would stand in front of it in silence. If it was a monastery, church, temple, or place of worship, I would close my eyes and feel the sound of the bells. I could feel the Spirit inside me praying with them. I could hear the voices of children, and the voices of men and women. The past always brings me back to sadness. I hear the crying of children and the cries of women who lost their children and their men. In these places I always feel the spirits of our ancestors.

When I sail in ancient places that are still inhabited by the spirits of our ancestors, I feel that I derive spirit, strength and passion from the strength of our ancestors, from the monks, the priests, the elders and the saints. Unfortunately, while I feel the spirit, I hear from behind the hills the sound of horses and battles and the sounds of arrows, swords and catapults as they destroyed those places and spread blood everywhere. I pledged to myself to spread peace, love and tolerance, and to one day speak about the history of Syria, the cradle of civilizations and the various religions here.

S: I have been touched by the prayers you offer during the Global Prayer Gathering. One of your prayers was, "My prayers are with all of yours to nourish the souls of all who live lives of suffering and in war. My prayers are with your prayers to give them the energy that gives them hope." What is the source of your faith?

Hasan: The source of my faith comes from Judaism and the worship of "God." I return to Judaism of 170 year ago, and from my embrace of the Islamic religion, and from the qualities of God in the Christian religion, and in all other religions. The source of my faith emanates from love, peace and tolerance found in all religions.

S: Your resourcefulness creating livable conditions for over 650 people, primarily women and children in refugee camps, is awe-inspiring. Please describe the camps, the farms, the schools for children.

Hasan: My help for others begins with the realization that wherever you are, you must grow and blossom. I always feel that I am like a seed. This seed must grow wherever it is planted and give us good crops and results. I see that whoever does not have goodness in the land in which he lives will have no goodness in any place he goes. Success begins always within yourself, your heart, then your room, then your house, then from the neighborhood in which you live, your city, your country, then around the world.

When the Syrian revolution began, from the first moments, I saw how civilians were being killed and that women and children were being arrested. I decided to work to achieve justice and hold the criminals accountable. This forced me to flee to the Turkish-Syrian border where I witnessed very bad conditions in camps and people living in terrible poverty.

I was an official spokesman for Syrian refugees inside and outside of

Syria. I was a witness for everyone who was forcibly displaced, some under the name of international sponsorship, and some for the sake of international interests. I started working for the refugees and demanded that the bombing stop.

I decided to start by changing the conditions of the tent camps where we lived. The first step was to start educating the children. During the war, they did not receive any education, so I established the Mariam School and I set out to teach the children.

Then, I became interested in making clothes and I bought sewing machines. After that, I decided to pay attention to the medical needs and established the first fixed dental clinic in northern Syria, and the first barbershop as well.

My attempts to succeed contended with my moments of collapse. I was collapsing from within. Then fate brought me together with Elisabeth. Elisabeth was the one person who gave me strength and hope in moments when I was collapsing in my heart as I tried to succeed but always faced difficulties.

Every day, the soup meal is the most important thing for the people of Mariam Camp. We provide bread and soup to the families in the Youssef, and to the Samaan Camps as well. We cultivate many family gardens and take care to make shade to alleviate suffering from the intense heat of living inside the tents.

We take care to teach women life-saving skills and how to deal with first aid in the event of accidents, fires, or injuries from bombings. We focus on educating children, raising their awareness, helping them integrate into society and how to demand their rights.

I always communicate to the children about love, tolerance and peace. Since we live in a society where customs and traditions prevail which limit the rights and freedoms of women and children, I want to give them positive knowledge that plants ideas of love and tolerance. For example, when I talk with the children about the different religions, we give them sweets or gifts. I try to plant seeds of love and respect in their hearts for different religions.

We celebrate different religious holy days. Our gardens are seen as signs of hope and salvation from death. Everything I talk about that we are able to do is thanks to the angel that God sent to us in the form of a human being, Elisabeth.

S: You and Elisabeth have an abiding friendship even though you live in a war zone in Syria, and she lives in a peaceful town in Austria. Elisabeth mentioned that God made a perfect match bringing you two together! Please share a few stories about projects you are proud of and problems you are solving together.

Hasan: Elisabeth standing with me to help the weak is my most important motivator. Also, my presence with the United Religions Initiative (URI) global team gives me the motivation to succeed and the strength to continue helping others and putting a smile on the faces of the weak.

If I talk about Elisabeth, I will not be satisfied with pages of written words. We talk almost every day about the things I need to do. Her friendship and help are something very special that I have witnessed in my life. She understands the suffering of children, women and the elderly, despite the thousands of kilometers that separate us.

To alleviate the suffering of others, she talks about her ideas within seconds of what I want to talk about. I realize again and again that she has abilities that differ from other humans, and she possesses knowledge that others in the rest of humanity do not know about.

The ideas here are about cultivating gardens and trees, providing skills and medical care, developing education and internet access for children. We address women's needs to give hope, spirit and optimism to alleviate their suffering and give them strength to be patient, to overcome sadness and to share hope for a better life.

S: Please share stories from the children and the mothers that inspire you. Is there an event or incident that will always stay in your heart?

Hasan: There is not one story, but many stories happen in front of me. We start with sadness when planes pass over, or bombings occur nearby. I always tell the children not to be afraid because the bullet you hear will not kill you. When you hear a sound, you must realize that you are still safe. To strengthen optimism, Elisabeth told me to teach technical things, so I explained to the children how a car engine works and how to fly a plane. One of the children told me, "I wish I could build a plane and shoot down those planes that are killing us."

When I presented shoes to women last year on International Women's Day, I told them that those shoes were given to honor the international day dedicated to women everywhere. Many women said to me out of sadness, "Do we have a day that the world celebrates?" We do not know about it." They said to me, "Thank you to those who remembered us and contributed by giving us a gift on a day that we do not know about and have never heard of before." There are many stories and things, the saddest of which is our country is in war.

S: You are such an excellent farmer! Your resourcefulness has turned arid, war-ravaged land into bountiful gardens providing abundant fruits and vegetables. What wisdom are you learning from gardening that you would like to pass along to the children in your camps and future generations?

Hasan: The wisdom of agriculture is that wherever you live you must plant and bear fruit. Agriculture gives the heart optimism and hope. Agriculture is a lifesaver for those living in areas of war and poverty. Agriculture gives hope to those who work in it. Farming gives you strength.

I always love children and take care of them as if they were seeds. If I water them with love and tenderness, they will be strong children, as will the trees and seeds. You should always water plants and trees with love and tenderness too before you water them with water, because plants and trees have souls inside them that feel us, and we must feel them as well.

S: Please share the story of building the flower garden in the center between the row of tents for the people who came to the camps after the earthquake.

Hasan: The idea is one of Elisabeth's. One of her dreams is to give every tent a flower garden. The idea was to make a basin of flowers for those who lost family members, lost everything, and were survived from the rubble of death. Elisabeth's idea was to make a flower bed in the middle of the tent rows to give the survivors hope and optimism again. I thank everyone who contributed to us and supported our work with all my heart. The people who built that hope were those who donated to this effort in the name of www.bildung-frieden.net.

When the people saw the gardens growing, their response was to give thanks from the bottom of their hearts. They cried tears of sadness for the loss of people dear to their hearts and also tears of hope mixed with thanks to everyone who contributed, putting a smile on their faces.

S: I know you have dreams for the children in the camps to have good and successful lives and that you also have your own aspirations that extend beyond your current work in Syria. What are the dreams you have for yourself?

Hasan: I have many dreams for Syria. I hope to establish the first house of worship for all religions in Syria. On a personal and professional level, I am an electrical engineer and I hope to be an inventor. I will allocate the money from my inventions to help others in developing countries and countries at war.

I want to study all religions. Traveling around the world sharing ideas about helping others from Elisabeth's and my experiences, teaching, making peace, building projects and working to help others around the world, under the name www.bildung-frieden.net.

S: I love your dreams for yourself and for Syria. May your dreams be fulfilled! So many people everywhere in the world yearn for a better life with more peace, prosperity and goodwill towards one another. What would you say to them to give them strength and guidance?

Hasan: I would tell them to work patiently. Be patient and work. If there is failure, failed attempts will be followed by success. You should not despair. Be patient and work. The first thing when you decide to work for your country is that you must believe in yourself and stick to your goals no matter how others bring you down. Don't look at the losers. Don't sit with them. The homeland is like a mother embracing her children, so work without despair, and be optimistic every day for the best. The light will remove the darkness, and the light we have always dreamed of will come.

About Hasan

Hasan grew up in Aleppo, one of 13 brothers and sisters from one mother. The eldest, Abu Bakr, died in childhood. His living siblings are Matt Taham, an electrical engineer; Abu Bakr, a carpenter; Hamza, a contractor; Omar, a teacher; Mahmoud, a teacher; Muhaymin, a student; Halima, a housewife; Mona a teacher; Asma a teacher; Aisha a teacher; and Sumaya, a teacher.

Hasan was educated as an electrical engineer and worked for an electric company in Aleppo. During the war, he became an official spokesman for refugees in and outside of Syria and dedicates his life to protecting and sustaining the lives of increasing numbers of refugees in three camps near Aleppo. In the camps he invents what is needed, manages huge farms, repairs broken machines, manages kitchens, educates, creates libraries, supplies medical needs, problem solves and gives people courage and hope to fulfill their aspirations.

His hobbies are collecting postage stamps and old coins, and his favorite game is chess.

He has a dream called "The Peace Cry" that he intends to realize one day. People from all over the world will be invited to scream one big cry for peace at the same time. "The Peace Cry" will happen on a specific day and time and will last a minute. "The Peace Cry" will raise up the voices of the weak and their sound will move the criminals to stop the killing. Hasan says, "I want the palaces of the criminals to be penetrated by our screams."

Luz Navarrette Chumakari

Caring is important, the heart you are talking about is important, so people feel that kind of connection. I didn't yell at them; I came across with the sincere feeling that I love you.

Luz prays every morning and evening that she hears what is being asked of her and that she obeys.

I met Luz several years ago when she did Spanish English interpretation for an indigenous gathering organized by the United Religions Initiative (URI). I remember Luz's discomfort when she was asked to interpret for an indigenous woman from Brazil who spoke Portuguese, not Spanish. After a few minutes together the Indigenous woman said, "Don't worry, Luz and I don't need to speak the same language we understand one another through Spirit." And so, they did!

Even though Luz and I had not connected for many years, I had a clear intuitive nudge to invite her to be interviewed for this book. Not knowing me well either, she felt the nudge of Spirit in my invitation and agreed. We met in her welcoming home graced by ancient oak trees and an enchanting garden tended by her husband Ricardo. Luz counsels and offers guidance in a special room that glows with art, and is a room of prayer dedicated to Our Lady of Guadalupe.

Luz conveys joyful confidence in the realm of spirit and the ancestors that direct her life. She believes that humanity is being called to a shift in consciousness that is bringing us closer to Mother Earth and allowing us to come together around the world as brother and sister. She felt in her heart that this foretold shift was predicted when she served as interpreter for global indigenous elders. Listening to her inner voice and asking for help from the realm of Spirit, Luz prays every morning and evening that she hears what is being asked of her and that she obeys.

SANTA CLARA UNIVERSITY
SANTA CLARA UNIVERSITY

S: Luz, I think you and I both want to express ideas that we've held inside ourselves. For me, it's the idea that democracy calls forth an inner, spiritual dimension in people. I remember your connection with Spirit and your light; I think you are a people person who is already living in this way. Please tell me about your upbringing that helped you become aligned with Spirit.

Luz: I was born that way. I was born with Spirit. My mother and father told me that when I was still in the crib a friend came to visit. His name was Angel. When he came in, I stood up and held out my hand and asked him, "Are you my guardian angel?" I was waiting for him. As a little child I already knew. My father and mother were surprised, and they and Angel smiled and thought that it was very sweet of me to think of him as a guardian angel.

I grew up with a sense of knowing the realm of Spirit and I was comfortable in that realm. When I was eight years old, we moved from Mexico to California, and I went to Catholic school. The first thing that got me thinking was going to Catholic Mass. We were told that girls could not go beyond the communion rail to the altar. I could not understand why this was so. One day during recess I went into the church, crossed the altar rail, went up to the altar and pretended I was saying Mass. Then I went to the pulpit and pretended that I was giving the sermon. I realized that nothing bad happened to me. God didn't punish me, and I started to think that they just made all that up.

When we had to prepare for Holy Communion, I was in line waiting with the other children to go into Confession. They were nervous and talking about what sins they would say. When I went in, I told the priest, "I talk to God every day. God knows everything I do, so I don't think I need to tell you anything because God already knows me."

That priest knew me and said, "That's ok if God already knows you, you don't have to tell me, just say a Hail Mary." That was it! He understood me and gave me permission to continue my personal relationship with God.

As I grew older, I appreciated the freedom to keep my relationship with Spirit and not let worldly rules block it from me. During the summer, my mother and father could not afford a babysitter and they would send me and my younger brother back to San Francisco del Oro in Mexico to stay with my grandmother, Chayito and my nina, Ana Maria. When I was there, I became enamored with the Rarámuri people. They were the native people who lived in the Sierra Madre. I just loved to see them. They would come into town and tie up their horses in front of my grandmother's house. They were beautiful people with smooth bronze skin, who dressed in manta attire (rough tan cotton). The men wore shorts and the women long skirts with red designs. They tied colorful woven sashes around their waist and a decorated bandana on their head, which kept their long, beautiful shiny black hair in place.

After selling their goods in town, they would head back to their village and would walk up to the hills and spend the night in the caves just out of town. I could see their fires in the caves at night. I always wondered what they were doing, wishing that I could join them.

In the early morning, I would wake my friend Chayo and we would hike up to the cave. We would go inside where we could still smell embers from the fire. The Rarámuri had already left but I sat in the cave closing my eyes and hoping that something special might happen. I felt the spirit of their presence and it made me happy.

When I was in Mexico, I heard stories about people dying in the mines and how their spirits came back after they crossed over. I grew up with a strong belief that spirits were around—not bad things about them—just a belief that spirits were around. My grandmother and aunt shared those beliefs.

My grandmother spoke Tepehuán, the native language of her tribe. I didn't learn the language, but she spoke certain words which I didn't recognize as Spanish. My brother and I returned to El Oro every summer.

Once I started to go to the university, I had to work in the summers to help pay my tuition. I attended Loyola Marymount University, and the tuition was very high. I didn't go back to Mexico during those summers, but I stayed connected to my family and friends.

I met Ricardo when I was a freshman in college when I was 17.

S: **I would love to know how you met Ricardo.**

Luz: I was very much into hair at the time, and I had bleached my hair and dyed it green. There was a group of Mexicanos who worked landscaping at the university. In the evening, they would gather on the quad to play their guitars and sing. I enjoyed hanging out and singing with them.

Ricardo would get out of class at 9pm and one day he noticed me sitting with these guys. He was curious as to who I was. He came up to me and asked my name, and then he asked if he could walk me to the dorms. He was also wondering where I was from. I said, "I am actually from Mars, don't you see my green hair?" He said, "So you are from Mars." I said "Yes, that's where I'm from."

We kept walking and he asked where my father and mother were from, I said they were from Mars as well. His response was OK. We walked to the dorm. Later he kept inviting me to do things with him, or just hang out. Even back then I felt I was from Mars, some place other than planet Earth. People were doing a lot of drug tripping in those days. Some of my friends would comment that, "She doesn't have to do any drugs, she is already in another world, another realm."

Every summer I worked at the university. In my junior year Ricardo was ready to go to graduate school. He was a great writer and great man, and the Jesuits loved him very much. They offered him a master's degree fellowship to stay and teach in the literature department. So, he stayed at the college and our relationship continued to grow.

Because I couldn't pay for both tuition and the dorm, I moved back with my parents my junior year. My parents were very strict and wouldn't let me stay out past 9 o'clock. I told Ricardo that we would have to get married because my parents wouldn't let me go on dates with him. I wanted to go to Mexico and travel with him. In his apartment there was a map on the wall, and he had shown me all the places where he wanted to travel. I told him that I would love to go with him, but I knew there was no way my parents would let me go.

I told my parents that we were going to get married. In our family it is a tradition for the groom's father to come and ask for the bride's hand in marriage. In our case that meeting was a formal dinner at my house. Ricardo's father and mother attended. His father told my parents about Ricardo's positive traits and how he would be a great husband. In turn my father told Ricardo's parents what a wonderful and gifted woman Ricardo would be marrying. The dinner went very well, and both of our parents were happy for us.

I told my parents that Ricardo wanted to meet my grandmother and all my relatives in Mexico. That summer we traveled in his Datsun pickup, even boarding a train across the Sierra Madre, where the Rarámuri live. When we came back, we planned our wedding, which took place in December. We had a very big and beautiful wedding with a Mariachi Mass followed by a reception with a Latin jazz band. In the evening, we had a big dance at a popular dance hall in Los Angeles with a top band playing top songs and oldies.

The following year we worked and saved our money because we had plans to travel through Mexico and Central America.

In 1976 we left for Mexico in a Datsun truck with a camper. Right before we left, I found out that I was pregnant with our first child. We decided not to tell anyone, otherwise they would be worried and concerned. We traveled and camped by rivers, the ocean and national parks. We headed to Central America but couldn't go to El Salvador because the border patrol informed us there was a revolution going on there. They warned us that if we crossed the border, the revolutionaries would take our camper.

We decided to return to Guadalajara and visit a Jesuit university there. They were offering a summer counseling program. Ricardo and I made an appointment to meet with the director. When they learned of Ricardo's educational background, they asked him to participate and then offered him a job in the counseling department. By this time, I was nine months pregnant, and we decided to come back to the U.S. It was just two weeks before our first daughter was born. She was born September 15, Mexican Independence Day. Her name is Luz de Alba, the "light at dawn" because she was born during dawn hours.

Upon our return Ricardo accepted a job with a community organization in Los Angeles. I was hired as a part time counselor in the neighborhood State Employment office where I made sure that farmworkers who had moved to the city received training and were placed in jobs. It wasn't long before we realized that we did not want to raise our daughter or future family in Los Angeles. Ricardo applied for counseling positions and accepted a job at West Valley College in Saratoga. I accepted a job as director of a high school counseling program for truant students. I also enrolled in a master's program in Counseling and Mexican American Studies. Our children, Sol de Otoño, Ricardi Angel and Estrella de Guadalupe were born in 1978, 1980, 1982.

One year Ricardo and I decided to go on a getaway weekend north to Santa Rosa to experience wine country. I didn't know such a beautiful place existed. The river reminded me of the village in Mexico where I grew up. I saw little girls in their Sunday dresses walking in the Healdsburg Plaza with their families. I told Ricardo, "We need to move here!"

Ricardo applied for a counseling position at Santa Rosa Junior College.

I still remember the day we went to drop off his application. We were walking on campus and saw a beautiful sprinkling fountain. Our son, Angel looked up at Ricardo and said, "Papá you need to get a job here!" A man was walking by and heard Angel. Patting him on the head, he said to Angel, "Maybe your Papá will get a job here." Ricardo was offered and accepted the job.

As my children still needed me at home, I applied for a part time counselor position. We rented a house until we found a beautiful forest property where we built our home. I continued to work in counseling programs, and it was gratifying to be able to help students get into college. Working with underrepresented students was a mission for both Ricardo and me. We continued our work for over 30 years.

When Estrella got sick, I was coordinating a statewide program called "Puente Program." When Estrella presented unusual symptoms, I already knew that she was going to be very sick.

The way it came to me … she was very sick and a woman who was my partner in the Puente Program told me that her son was sick with similar symptoms, and the doctors thought he had leukemia. When I heard the word "leukemia" I knew immediately that is what Estrella had. Later, I told Ricardo, and he didn't want to believe it.

Once Estrella was diagnosed and in the hospital, I never left her side. I was there the whole time, day and night. I realized that I was not only at the hospital for Estrella, but I was also there for other children and their moms. I was there to teach them how to do energetic healing work with their hands to help their children heal.

Estrella read hundreds of books. The police and fire departments gave her money to buy books because she was reading the whole time and having a calm experience. This was before laptop computers.

Sol, her brother, turned out to be a perfect match for a bone marrow transplant. The transplant was very successful, and she came back to life. Estrella enjoyed reading mystery books by R.L. Stine. I wrote to tell him that my daughter loved reading his books and on her 12th birthday, December 12th, the anniversary of our Lady of Guadalupe, he sent her a collection of his books with his autograph. She was so happy to receive such a special birthday gift.

In January she was rollerblading around her school campus. Suddenly, she sat down on the ground and looked up at me and said, "Mom, I can't do this anymore." I asked, "What do you mean?" She said, "I just can't be here anymore, I need to go to the other place." I asked why and she said, "It's just time for me to go." She soon developed a high fever and we had to take her to the hospital.

The "Make a Wish Foundation" came and asked her to make a wish. She said, "You know, big buildings and libraries are named after rich old men, and there aren't any buildings named for a little girl. I want a library named after me." That's what she said. Her teacher from school said, "You know we are going to make that happen. We are going to have the school library named the "Estrella Library."

She was so happy! Her teacher made sure the library was named after her.

S: What a wonderful thing to ask for.

Luz: She was always reading so it was perfect to have the library named after her. But after she crossed over, she began communicating with me. She was telling me to do this and directing me to do that and I was following her orders. She told me where she wanted a bench in the library and how to decorate it. She wanted pillows made with stars on them. She kept on connecting with me in that specific way.

When it was time for me to go back to work, I told her I couldn't keep communicating with her like this. She said, "OK, but we will keep on connecting"—we still connect with each other every day.

S: How do you connect?

Luz: It is an understanding that comes into my mind. I don't hear her voice, but I know that she is speaking with me.

I have other friends who have crossed over. I don't hear their voices, but I know they are communicating with me. There is a lot of humor in it.

When I went back to work, I learned about a presentation in Ireland on "Spirituality in the Classroom." I sensed that Estrella wanted me to submit the application. I had never presented outside of the United States but really felt compelled to do it. I applied and was selected to be a presenter at that conference. As I prepared, I started getting visions.

I have a little Mayan figurine that is hollow in the middle with another little figure inside the hollow belly area. I used it to tell my students that we all have an inner guide. We each have a spiritual being that guides us, and we need to be in tune with that being, the spirit inside of us.

I was driving one day with my son Angel when I saw a vision of what the cover page of my presentation would be: the little figurine with a spiraling energy coming out of its center. I was so happy that this image and idea came to me.

Angel and Ricardo accompanied me to Ireland. After my presentation, we went to visit an ancient site. When we got there, we saw a big stone in front of the site. The stone had a carving of that same spiraling image.

I said to Angel, "What do you see?" he said, "Oh my god Mom, that is the same image that came to you." We toured around Ireland, and I connected with spiritual women. It was a powerful experience, and when I came back home this realm had opened for me even more. I knew I had to listen and obey when I was asked to do something. Obey.

S: Is that when you began to bring your connection to the spirit realm into your teaching?

Luz: There were many experiences that guided me. I was informed about a gathering of indigenous leaders in Mexico. I contacted the Mayan elder organizing it and said, "I am not an elder from an indigenous community, but I want to come to this gathering." He said, "Yes, you can come and interpret for the elders." So, I went to the Yucatan in Mexico.

As soon as I arrived, I started interpreting for the elders. I met a Native American elder with a limp who needed help walking and carrying his bag. We became friends.

Native American women were in attendance, but they were not being given a chance to speak. When I listened to what was going on, it was the women who were saying the important stuff, not the men. I totally got that! Maybe that was why they were not being given a chance to speak, because they were coming up with ideas that I thought were very important.

I was hanging out with the elder, interpreting. We heard that there was a man at the gathering who was an imposter, not a native representative.

We were gathered under a huge tent. I was sitting close to the same elder for whom I was interpreting. The man whom the elder believed to be an imposter was going to speak, but then the ropes holding down the tent began to unwind on their own. Suddenly, this huge tent was airlifted. It started going round one way and then the other and then collapsed. The elder pulled me out. The tent landed on the guy who was the imposter and knocked him out. They had to revive him.

The elder put his arm around me and said, "Don't be afraid, I knew this was going to happen, I knew that guy was not telling the truth."

When we were talking about the gifts that people had, he told me that his was the gift of the wind, and that it was this gift that had caused the wind to unravel the ropes and make the tent fall. He reassured me that I would be fine. I got to experience that and that was powerful!

I developed a personal connection with that group of indigenous elders. The leaders from the group told me that I walk alone. Even though I have my husband and my family, they said my journey on Earth is to walk alone, to do a spiritual walk alone.

Many messages come to me in dreams. I do dream work, and I was at a dreamwork conference when I met a shaman elder from Africa. He did a reading with me and said the same thing, "You are to work alone." He said, "You need to get out into the world. You don't really have to do much; your work will come to you." I have had people tell me these things. Now he has crossed over into the other realm and I am still here trying to figure out how this is all going to manifest.

S: Do you hear messages from the people who have passed over about what people on Earth need to do differently? How can more people open to connecting with the spirit realm?

Luz: I think that you need to believe. You need to have faith and you need to believe in this realm of beings. When I was going to church, they told me you can't do this and that. I had to find out for myself.

I've always had a very curious spirit. I don't have fear of something bad happening to me because I feel that I am very well protected by many powerful beings in the other realm. I know that and I just feel that. You can't mess with that protection.

Having faith – when Estrella crossed over, I knew that she didn't leave like we usually think about death, because after she crossed over, she started telling me all these things that I had to move on and do. I know that she didn't die. She still communicates with me!

In my morning prayer time, I talk with other good friends who have crossed over, my wonderful mechanic and the dean of the college, bless her heart. The dean had given me the freedom to do whatever I needed to do to help the students. She trusted my judgment and gave me that freedom. The blessing is that I have always been given the permission and the tools to do the work that I need to do. It is hard work, not easy work. The work that I have done has been time and energy consuming. I continue to do it because I feel that I am guided and supported in that way.

I went to the Copper Canyon where my ancestors on my father's side lived. I always felt that calling. The Rarámuri people live there. The same people that as a child I had fallen in love with. As I researched the family tree, I discovered that my father's mother was Rarámuri. It is the ancestral connection that led me to the Copper Canyon so that I could connect with my Rarámuri family. I met Teresita, a leader of the Rarámuri community and I asked her if she could make a traditional dress for me. As I told her my story, she assured me that I am a relative, a family member.

One year on the spring equinox, the same day as Estrella's crossing, I was invited to come to their community. Only Rarámuri are allowed to go there. Teresita made me a beautiful traditional dress, which I was to wear for my baptism and welcoming into the Rarámuri family. I have been baptized and accepted into the Raramuri community. The Rarámurii shaman elders oversee and protect my work from a distance. They pray so that people here who need help are guided to me.

The elder said to me that you don't have to worry about what happens to you. I have the ability to leave my body and travel and I am overseeing you. So, wherever you are I can be there—so you don't need to worry.

S: I wonder what indigenous wisdom says about where we are now as a human race. It seems like we are at a critical point. I wonder what their wisdom is for these times.

Luz: It depends where you are. When I am down there in the caves with the tribal people . . . I am just there as a shepherd girl taking care of the animals and being with the fire in the caves. Everything there is real. The fires, the food they are cooking. The cave is cold and when it is raining you see lightning and thunder just outside the cave. It is powerful! Lightning vibrating in the caves. When I am there, I experience a tremendous feeling of freedom. Life is very simple. They have corn to eat, water from creeks and the river. When I am there, I don't worry about anything, we have just what we need. When I think about the world out there, I realize how crazy it is. It is crazy. All I can do is pray. Pray.

There are prophecies that have been spoken about.

S: Is there a prophecy that you think is especially important?

Luz: I don't think about prophecies much. I have been to the Hopis and met the man who wrote, "The Hopi Survival Kit." I was with his family and spoke with him. I have this connection with the people in this other realm that gives me the confidence not to stress myself out about what is going on globally in the world and even locally with drug issues and all the violence. I think this has been going on forever. It is something that is part of this planet that we live on. I don't think it is going to go away.

In my classes I teach people to do what I do . . . to connect with the realm of higher spirit, to listen to the guidance and obey what they are being asked to do. That is a hard thing. Sometimes the things you hear don't make sense.

S: **Your experiences reveal that there is so much more going on beyond the physical world. How can we help people to experience this higher consciousness?**

Luz: Yes, we need to be open to it. We need to be open to that other realm and believe that we are coexisting within that realm, and that it connects us to people and to places. We need to acknowledge it. When Ricardo and I were on vacation in Mexico, we met an artist and saw a painting in her gallery that looked just like a picture of Estrella. She told us it was her niece. She told us that her name was Estrella. We all started crying because we couldn't believe it. Wow—we were so deeply connected through the painting of her niece, who looked just like Estrella! That was very powerful. Experiences like this happen here and there and I just kind of wait for the next one to happen.

S: **I notice that you tell your own stories in your teaching. I'm seeing how important it is to learn from people's stories, not just reading theories about a metaphysical dimension, but hearing personal experiences.**

Luz: My students always want me to tell them stories; I have all kinds of stories to tell. My experiences walking the Camino de Compostela . . . all that Ricardo and I have lived though and continue to experience.

I've been told that I should start a podcast because I have stories to tell. People want to hear my stories. Students say they miss my stories. Maybe I'll start a podcast soon. I love to tell stories!

S: **Let me ask you about this deeper meaning of democracy. I'm curious to learn about how democracy gives people the freedom to make decisions from their heart.**

Luz: I relate it to experiences with my students. Kids and families are having problems now, especially at the high school level. Ricardo and I have always provided opportunities for people who didn't have equitable resources.

Recently, my daughter, a high school teacher, invited me to her classroom. There was a girl in her class who was 'acting out' and I told her I needed to talk to her and took her out into the hall. I said, "I don't have to be here. I'm here because my daughter thinks it might be good for me to share some information that might be helpful to you." I told her, "I'm here because I love you."

When I said that she started crying and said, "You love me, you love me?" I gave her a hug.

She started crying. She said, "You don't know me." I said, "I love you." She was overwhelmed. I said, "You don't have to be here with me, you can go to the library or some other place. I can give you a pass to go somewhere else."

Another class came in. This time it was a boy and he started 'acting out' the same way. I took him into the hall and said the same thing, "You don't have to be here, and I don't have to be here either. I'm here because I love you." When I said that he started crying, and I hugged him. I said, "It's ok, hearing the words 'I love you' from someone you don't even know. It doesn't happen often, but I do love you, and I'm committed to be here to say things to you that are going to help you prepare to go to college." I said, "You don't have to come tomorrow; you can go to the library, or whatever and it will be fine." He went back to the classroom. The next day they both came back to the class and stuck it out for the whole semester.

Caring is important, the heart you are talking about is really important for people to feel that kind of connection. I didn't yell at them; I came across with the sincere feeling that "I love you." That is not something that they are used to hearing. I think that applies everywhere we go.

S: **That story brings up the idea of moving "from head to heart." Your words, "I love you, I want to engage with you because I love you" are radical.**

Luz: You see so many people getting hurt. There are risks people take when they open up their heart. You could say it is a risky thing to open your heart.

S: One last question. When you think of your children, grandchildren, and your students, are there guiding words you want to offer to help them in life?

Luz: It is important to show you care. To show love that comes from giving care. You must be a loving person most of all.

When you get into your head it can play tricks on you, so lots of times when my mind is playing games with me, I need to take a deep breath . . . and go inside myself and listen to this deep part of myself and listen to what it is saying. I teach students how to do that.

The overwhelming situation on planet Earth just calls me to offer prayer. I feel that when I pray, I'm putting out intentions for whatever my prayers can do. When I pray, I feel like I am doing something towards whatever is the specific intention of my prayer. When I hear the news, I give an intention of prayer and send it out.

When I am asked to do something from the realm of spirit, I need to have three confirmations. When they come, I go ahead and do what I'm being asked. Obedience is not easy to do.

I didn't tell you this story. I don't know how it is all going to fit in.

I was on a retreat in New Mexico with shamans and doctors of medicine. We were doing a shamanic journey to connect with the other realm to find remedies for breast cancer and other diseases. When I was there, I connected with a woman doctor from New York who had helped people crossover during the 9/11 blasts.

One night I felt that there was a presence in my room, I told a doctor that I felt a presence like a person in my room. He said, "Sometimes people commit suicide in hotel rooms. Maybe there was a spirit there that hasn't left." I said, "Don't tell me that, I don't want to hear that part of it."

The next day I asked that doctor and the woman doctor from New York to come into my room to see if they could feel anything. They walked in and said, "Luz, there is a huge presence in this room. A huge presence!" We decided to pray. I lit a candle and we started to pray. This woman doctor told me, "Estrella is here in this room and there are others coming—your whole family is coming and filling the room. They are all here now and they are surrounding you here."

I was overwhelmed. Then these revelations started to come like a movie playing . . .

Boom, I just fell on the bed. He went to my feet and the woman doctor went to my head to ground me. I was seeing lots of things like a movie playing…and I watched all these things happening for three hours. I was exhausted. She said, "I think it is over." I went to lay down and said, "No more revelations." I wanted to sleep.

When I woke up the next morning I wasn't feeling so well. It was the last day of the conference. After I checked out, the hotel called me and told me that I had left my purse. I went back and the front desk clerk, who was Mexican, spoke to me in Spanish. He told me that when he first came to work, he got cancer in his cheek. It was bad but a spirit came and told him that he could heal himself by putting his hand on his cheek.

He told me, "You have a gift. You had to come back to get your purse because you needed to be reminded to use that gift." He said that to me.

I left and thought that was interesting! The elder told me to eat a lot of fruit to help me process what had happened to me, they called it "a download.'"I don't know, I got a lot of information for three hours about a lot of things.

It was more like an historical movie of things that happened on Earth. It was a lot…and I said that I didn't want to receive more information. This is it for now.

The shamans who have guided me told me that people will come to me. I don't have to do anything, the people will come.

I am taking care of my father now; he is 97 years old. At this time, I am planning to join my daughter Luci, granddaughter Lucelina and grandson Diego to walk the Camino de Compostela in Spain. This will be my third time. The first time was with my husband Ricardo, my son Angel and myself. The second time I walked it with my son Sol. This time will be my last as our family will have completed the sacred journey in honor of Estrella.

S: Thank you, Luz, that is a beautiful way to end our conversation.

About Luz

Over ten years ago Luz was adopted into the Rarámuri tribal family in the Copper Canyon of Chihuahua Mexico and given the name Chumakari. Chumakari means "mother of water" and Rarámuri means "nimble feet." Luz remains close with her tribal sister Teresita, visits the village when she can and follows indigenous ways, walking and praying in nature and calling on the spirit world for guidance.

Luz built a profession as a counselor and teacher at Santa Rosa Junior College in Santa Rosa, California. Luz and her husband Ricardo dedicated their educational careers to working heart to heart and with respect for each student. They reminded students of their dreams, championed equal opportunity for all students, and led them to fulfill their potential by believing in them.

For over 22 years Luz has inspired and led local citizen committees of Sonoma County in a huge community event celebrating the traditional Día de los Muertos (Day of the Dead). Over the years it has evolved into a multi-cultural civic event that weaves together an economically and culturally diverse community with love and mutual respect.

When Luz moved to the U.S. from Mexico, she was eight and attended elementary school. Her first report card read "remedial." Luz was worried and didn't understand what that meant as she was always on top of her class in Mexico. Luz's mother told her, "You are just so far ahead of everyone else they don't know how to grade you." Luz is still far ahead but now people are responding to her special gifts—her voice is being called into action.

"When you get into your head it can play tricks on you, so lots of times when my mind is playing games with me, I need to take a deep breath . . . and go inside myself and listen to this deep part of myself and listen to what it is saying.

Afterword and Gratitude

Serendipity was explained to me as the surprising and significant things that happen along the journey to your destination. My journey compiling this book would not be complete without acknowledging the providential serendipities that showed up along the way.

Inspiration and people appeared right on time! I was inspired to enrich the unfolding story of democracy through people's authentic experiences, not philosophy. Conducting and transcribing these interviews, touching each person's character and way of being, filled me with energy, admiration and hope. It was a journey of mutual discovery. When we ask others to tell their stories and we listen with our heart, we uncover the wholeness to which we all belong. In this way we use our 'people power' wisely and grow together.

My deepest gratitude goes to everyone's willingness to participate generously in the production of this book. *The Global Heart of Democracy* was enriched immensely when Dan Holmgren, CEO of Imagemakers, Inc., chose to walk this journey with me and donated his superb enhanced photographic images. I'm grateful for Carl Brune's warm book design, funding help from many friends, and the confidence and courage inspired in me by Paulette Millichap, Dee Stump, Sheri Ritchlin, Mary and Jim Manning and my daughters, Katie and Lizzie Ackerly.

Bibliography

My desire to propel a globally connected heart-centered democracy is grounded in the writings of thought leaders, pathfinders and spirit-led civic leaders. This brief bibliography opens a footpath on a journey of discovery. I hope the selections included in this bibliography will inspire you to be purveyors of a spiritual democracy born from your yearning for a better world.

1. *Across that Bridge, Life Lessons, and a Vision for Change,* John Lewis, Hatchette Books, USA, 2012

   Spiritual integrity blazed within the heart of John Lewis (1940–2020), a long-term U.S. Congressman and renowned U.S. civil rights leader, whose moral conscience ignited the best in American democracy.

   > "Why must we, as members of the human family, immerse ourselves in the agency of turmoil and unrest to affect the evolution of humankind? Why participate in the work of justice at all? Each of us must answer these questions according to the dictates of our conscience and the principles of our faith. I believe that we are all a spark of the divine, and if that spark is nurtured it can become a burning flame … I believe that the true destiny of humankind is to recollect that it is light and learn how to abide in infinite awareness of the divine in all matters of human affairs."

2. *The American Soul, Rediscovering the Wisdom of the Founders,* Jacob Needleman, Jeremy P. Tarcher/Putnam, USA, 2003

   Jacob Needleman (1934–2020), American philosopher, religious scholar, author, asked aching, human questions. In his book, *The American Soul, Rediscovering the Wisdom of the Founders,* he uncovered spiritual ideals embedded in the nascent story of democracy in America and affirmed the mighty source of "people power."

   > "The question is: can the ideals of democracy remind us that we need to become what John Dewey called democratic individuals: men and women who are inwardly democratic, who are able to step back from the personal emotions in order to allow the other to think and speak and live. Democracy, in this sense, refers not only to an outer form of government, but to a power within oneself."

3. *Mary P. Follett, Creating Democracy, Transforming Management,* Joan C. Tonn, Yale University Press, New Haven, USA and London, UK, 2003

    Mary Parker Follett (1868–1933), a U.S. philosopher, social reformer, pioneer in organizational theory, believed in the capacity of people to work creatively and cooperatively to solve problems. She saw that the human soul needs the nourishment of diverse thinking for its growth and recognized that a deeper spiritual energy is needed to accomplish collective problem solving.

    > "It takes more spiritual energy to express the group spirit than the particular spirit. This is its glory as well as its difficulty. We have to be a higher order of beings to do it—we become a higher order of being by doing it."

4. "Forgetting We Are Not God," a speech given by Vaclav Havel, Stanford University, March 1995

    Vaclav Havel (1936–2011) was a Czech playwright, poet, dissident and political leader. He served as the first president of the Czech Republic (1993–2003) and wrote numerous books that reveal the morality and compassion he brought to civic life. In speeches at Stanford University and to the U.S. Congress in the early 90s he spoke about democracy not only as a political system but also as a spiritual ideal that aligns humanity with the transcendent.

    > "Planetary democracy does not yet exist, but our global civilization is already preparing a place for it: It is the very Earth we inhabit, linked with Heaven above us. Only in this setting can the mutuality and the commonality of the human race be newly created, with reverence and gratitude for that which transcends each of us singly and all of us together."

5. *Courage to Live in a Dangerous World, the Political Writings of Eleanor Roosevelt,* edited by Allida M. Black, Columbia University Press, 2000

    Eleanor Roosevelt (1884–1962), a remarkable first lady of the U.S. and wife of President Franklin D. Roosevelt. Her historic accomplishment was to help write the Universal Declaration of Human Rights, completed in 1948. Eleanor had the spirit of democracy in her bones and in her heart.

    > "I still do believe that there is within most of us a basic desire to live uprightly and kindly with our neighbors, but I also feel that we are, at

present in the grip of a wave of fear that threatens to overcome us. I think
we need a rude awakening … to make us willing to sacrifice all that we
have from the material standpoint in order that freedom and democracy
may not perish from the Earth."

6. *Biosophy and Spiritual Democracy: A Basis for World Peace*, Dr. Frederick
Kettner, Second printing by the Biosophical Institute, 2003

Dr. Frederick Kettner (1886–1957), inspired by the philosopher Spinoza,
was a pioneer in teaching about the deeper nature of human beings. He
advocated a new kind of learning called Biosophy that aimed to develop
each person's spiritual intelligence. He saw that the accomplishments of
democracy were not an end but steps toward a greater goal where people
would truly realize democratic ideals.

> "We need heroic individuals who will dare to become spiritual pioneers
> and begin "the war to end all wars"—the revolution within themselves.
> It begins when an individual revolutionizes his orientation to life from
> a material one to a spiritual one and will put forth the effort to create
> new kinds of spiritual values by which other human beings can also
> begin to live. Such pioneers will be the vanguard to an advanced form of
> democracy—a spiritual democracy."

7. *The Open Space of Democracy*, Terry Tempest Williams, Orion Society, 2004,
Wipf and Stock, 2010

Terry Tempest Williams (1955–), raised in Utah, is a writer, philosopher,
naturalist and advocate for ecological consciousness and social justice. She
speaks passionately for principles and actions that spring from an ethical
stance toward all life. Writing *The Open Space of Democracy* in the aftermath of
9/11 when fear threatened to stifle open discussion and respect for "the other,"
her insights are trailblazers today.

> "The only space I see being truly closed is not the land or our civil liberties
> but our own hearts. The human heart is the first home of democracy. It
> is where we embrace our questions: can we be equitable? Can we be
> generous? Can we listen with our whole being, not just our minds; and
> offer our attention rather than our opinions? And do we have enough
> resolve in our hearts to act courageously, relentlessly, without giving up
> ever, trusting our fellow citizens to join with us in our determined pursuit
> of a living democracy?"

8. *Healing the Heart of Democracy, The Courage to Create a Politics Worthy of the Human Spirit,* Parker Palmer, Jossey-Bass Publisher, 2011

   Dr. Parker J. Palmer (1939–) is an educator, highly acclaimed writer and recipient of many awards honoring his leadership, social activism and profound respect for the human spirit. In 2021 he was awarded a Lifetime Achievement Award by the Freedom of Spirit Fund which "honors exemplary individuals embodying that inner freedom that is the energizing source of human courage, creativity and love for the world." He looks to the power of the human heart to guide people's decisions and actions toward a renewed democracy.

   > "Heart … is a word that reaches far beyond our feelings. It points to a larger way of knowing—of receiving and reflecting on our experience— that goes deeper than the mind alone can take us. The heart is where we integrate the intellect with the rest of our faculties, such as emotions, imagination and intuition. It is where we can learn to think the world together, not apart, and find the courage to act on what we know."

9. *Markings,* Dag Hammarskjold, Alfred Knopf Publisher and Faber and Faber LTD, 1964

   Dag Hammarskjold (1905–1961) died in airplane crash while flying to negotiate a cease-fire between the United Nations and the Katanga forces in Zimbabwe. In his lifetime he achieved national and international acclaim. He served as Chair of the Board of Governors for the Bank of Sweden, became a financial advisor and member of the Swedish delegation to the United Nations in 1948 and was selected Secretary General of the United Nations in 1957.

   Markings is his personal diary written during his years of public prominence. It provides a rare insight into the inner life of a global statesman and political leader. His writings wander from musings to prayers to biblical quotes and poetry. They reveal his humble service, vulnerability, commitment to the common good, and spiritual integrity. This short entry shows where his heart lies.

   > Give me a pure heart – that I may see Thee,
   > A humble heart – that I may hear Thee,
   > A heart of love – that I may serve Thee,
   > A heart of faith, that I may abide in Thee

www.ingramcontent.com/pod-product-compliance
Lightning Source LLC
Chambersburg PA
CBHW040754120726
48005CB00012B/1170